Virtual Lab Manual with CD

for

Goldstein's

Sensation and Perception

Virtual Lab Manual with CD

for

Goldstein's

Sensation and Perception

Seventh Edition

Janet Proctor
Purdue University

THOMSON
WADSWORTH

Australia • Brazil • Canada • Mexico Singapore • Spain • United Kingdom • United States

Printed in the United States of America
1 2 3 4 5 6 7 09 08 07 06 05

Printer: Thomson West

ISBN0-495-03179-8
Credit image: © Photo by Petronella Ytsma of Original artwork by Tim Harding "Oro y Rojo"

Thomson Higher Education
10 Davis Drive
Belmont, CA 94002-3098
USA

For more information about our products, contact us at:
Thomson Learning Academic Resource Center
1-800-423-0563

For permission to use material from this text or product, submit a request online at
http://www.thomsonrights.com.
Any additional questions about permissions can be submitted by email to **thomsonrights@thomson.com.**

Table of Contents

Intensity and Brightness
Inhibition and Mach Band
Simultaneous Contrast
Simultaneous Contrast: Static
Simultaneous Contrast: Dynamic
Simple Neural Circuits
Mapping Receptive Fields
Receptive Field Mapping
Stimulus Size and Receptive Fields
Receptive Fields and Stimulus Size and Shape
The Visual Pathways
Simple Cells in the Cortex
Complex Cells in the Cortex
Calculating Grating Contrast
Contrast Sensitivity
Orientation Aftereffect
Size Aftereffect
Spatial Vision

Global Precedence

Chapter 1: Introduction to Perception

Virtual Labs for Chapter 1:

Rabbit-Duck Demonstration
Young Girl-Old Woman
The Method of Limits
Measurement Fluctuation and Error
Adjustment and PSE
Method of Constant Stimuli
Measuring Illusions
DL by the Method of Limits
Just Noticeable Difference
Weber's Law and Weber Fraction
DL vs. Weight
Scaling Vision
Response Compression and Expansion

Rabbit-Duck Demonstration

The rabbit-duck figure represents a type of bistable figure. In a bistable figure, the perception of the figure changes. What might initially be perceived as a rabbit later is perceived as a duck, or vice versa. With continued observation, the process reverses again.

As you view this figure, pay attention to which version you perceive first (e.g., rabbit or duck) and how frequently your perception alternates. Note whether one version is more stable than the other. Also, try viewing the pictures sideways (rotate your head to the side) to see if the effect is the same from that position.

RESULTS & DISCUSSION

1. Report your first impression of the figure and the frequency with which it changed. Was one perception more stable than the other?

2. Some people initially have difficulty seeing one of the two identities. Did you experience that? Why do you think this occurs?

3. Most objects are still easily identified when they have been rotated to a sideways position. How did changing the orientation affect the figure? Why do you think this occurred?

Young Girl-Old Woman

The young girl-old woman figure represents another type of bistable figure. In a bistable figure, the identity of the figure changes. What might initially be perceived as a young woman later is perceived as an old woman. With continued observation, the process then reverses.

As you view this figure, pay attention to which version you perceive first (e.g., young woman or old woman) and how frequently your perception alternates. Note whether one version is more stable than the other. Also, try viewing the pictures sideways (rotate your head to the side) to see if the effect is the same from that position.

RESULTS & DISCUSSION

1. Report your first impression of the figure and the frequency with which it changed. Was one perception more stable than the other?

2. Some people initially have difficulty seeing one of the two identities. Did you experience that? Why do you think this occurs?

3. Most objects are still easily identified when they have been rotated to a sideways position. How did changing the orientation affect the figure? Why do you think this occurred?

The Method of Limits

The method of limits is one of Fechner's classical psychophysical methods used to examine how perception relates to stimulation. In the method of limits, stimuli are presented in ascending or descending order, with the observer making a response after each presentation. A stimulus series is continued until the response changes. At that point, a new series begins, usually in the opposite order. The point at which the observer's response changes provides information about the perceptual threshold.

As illustrated in this demonstration, the method of limits may be used to measure the absolute threshold, the minimum energy necessary for detection of a stimulus. The observer, Laszlo, responds either YES (detected the stimulus) or NO (did not detect the stimulus) to each stimulus presented. Click the number at the top of a series, and then click the PRESENT button to present a stimulus and have Laszlo generate a response. Repeat, completing each series. Note the point at which the response changes in each series. Be sure to click on the two buttons located below Laszlo.

RESULTS & DISCUSSION

1. Report the thresholds for each series and the overall estimate of the absolute threshold.

2. Explain what is meant by the error of habituation and how this problem is minimized in the method of limits.

3. Why were the thresholds different from series to series? Could this be a problem for the concept of threshold? Explain your answer.

Measurement Fluctuation and Error

In the method of adjustment demonstrated in this exercise, the observer, not the experimenter, manipulates the stimulus. The observer adjusts the magnitude of the stimulus until it is detected, or is no longer detected, or is perceived to be equal to another stimulus, depending on the threshold of interest. This might seem to be a more direct and more accurate way of obtaining information about perception. However, this exercise demonstrates that even such a direct measurement is prone to error and variability.

Use your cursor to adjust the red triangle until it appears to be the same size as the blue triangle. When you are satisfied that the two triangles are the same size, click on RESULT. After recording your result for a trial, click on NEXT TRIAL and repeat the procedure until you have completed 10 trials. Click on DATA to view a frequency distribution of your responses. Note the pattern of your responses.

RESULTS & DISCUSSION

1. Report your data, and describe the pattern of your errors.

2. Did your errors tend to decrease in magnitude across the 10 trials? What do you think accounts for this (whether or not you produced this pattern of responding)? Do you think this change reflects a change in perception, or a change in how the task is performed? Explain.

3. Explain what this demonstration teaches us.

Adjustment and PSE

The point of subjective equality (PSE) is the stimulus value at which a comparison stimulus is perceived to be equal to some standard stimulus. As you might suspect, given that there is a special measurement for this, observers do not always perceive two stimuli as equal, even when they *are* equal. Sometimes the observer's perceptual system is not adequate to discriminate small differences. Sometimes the context in which the stimulus is presented will influence perception, as in many geometric illusions of size.

The method of adjustment is used again in this exercise. Instead of the size of a triangle, however, you will work with line length. Note that the length of the adjusted line begins smaller on some trials and longer on others. Use your cursor to adjust the line's length. Click on RESULT when you are satisfied that the two lines are equal in length. Click on CALCULATE PSE to compute the point of subjective equality, and click on PLOT DATA to view a graph of your data. Clear the data and repeat the sequence.

RESULTS & DISCUSSION

1. Report your data for each set of the 20 trials and also your PSE and mean error for each set.

2. Were your errors equally distributed between positive and negative errors? Was your PSE more accurate for the second set of 20 trials? What might account for this?

3. Why do you think people make errors judging line lengths? After all, the two lines are right there in plain view.

Method of Constant Stimuli

In the method of constant stimuli procedure, stimuli are presented in pseudo-random order, rather than in the ordered series used in the method of limits. This procedure is considered more accurate than the method of limits or method of adjustment because it controls for some of their weaknesses.

In this exercise, the method of constant stimuli is used to obtain the DL for line length. A blue line of constant length is the standard stimulus, and a red line of variable length is the comparison stimulus. You should respond as to whether the red line is shorter or longer than the blue line. Below the stimulus you will see a record of which stimulus was presented and how many times it has been presented to that point.

Click on RESULTS when you have completed the exercise. You will see a table showing the frequency of each response for each stimulus, and these data are converted to proportions. The data are graphed, and the DL is obtained. Record your data. Note the new term, interval of uncertainty.

RESULTS & DISCUSSION

1. Report your data, and reproduce the graph using those data.

2. Why do you think 0.75 is used to define the stimulus value that represents the upper threshold? (Hint: If simply guessing, one of two possible responses would be expected to be made on 50% of trials.)

3. What is the interval of uncertainty? How is it used in the DL computation?

4. How does the method of constant stimuli improve upon the method of limits? Cite at least one difference and why it is an improvement.

Measuring Illusions

Perceptual illusions are interesting in their own right, but they also may provide good information about how the perceptual system works. As a result, researchers have tried to understand the origins of many perceptual illusions and the variables that affect them. In this experiment you have the opportunity to measure the strength of three illusions under different conditions and to see how the method of limits is used in real research. The three illusions are the Muller-Lyer illusion, the vertical-horizontal illusion, and simultaneous brightness contrast.

In each version of this experiment you will be asked to make a YES-NO judgment comparing two stimuli. Be sure to pay attention to the question being asked, and don't miss the briefly presented stimulus. Also, wait until the YES and NO buttons are no longer dimmed, or your response will not register. Print out your data for each condition and each illusion, and save it to a file until you have completed this exercise.

Muller-Lyer Illusion

One factor thought to influence the Muller-Lyer illusion is misleading depth information. By manipulating the length of the arrowheads on the ends of the lines, the impact of the linear perspective depth cue may be emphasized or diminished. If the illusion does involve misperceived depth, manipulating the depth cue should change the illusion magnitude. Your task here is to decide whether the top line is longer than the bottom line.

RESULTS & DISCUSSION

1. Report your data for each condition. Did the illusion magnitude vary as the length of the arrowheads changed? Did it increase or decrease?

2. Do your results support the inappropriate size-distance (depth) scaling theory of the Muller-Lyer Illusion? Why or why not?

3. Why do you think the two illusion figures were offset when presented and presented for only a few seconds? Is this a good idea?

Measuring Illusions, continued
Vertical-Horizontal Illusion

One view of the vertical-horizontal illusion suggests that the bisection of the horizontal line by the vertical line in the standard illusion figure is the primary cause of the illusion. In this experiment you will be able to test this theory. The TOP condition presents the vertical line above and separate from the horizontal line. The BOTTOM condition presents the vertical line in the standard position, bisecting the horizontal line. Your task is to respond whether the vertical line is longer than the horizontal line. Be sure to wait until the response buttons are activated before you respond, and be ready for the briefly presented stimuli. Print out and save your data for each condition.

RESULTS & DISCUSSION

1. Report your data for each presentation condition. Was the illusion magnitude larger or smaller when the vertical line was not touching the horizontal line? (You have not performed the necessary statistics to allow a scientific conclusion concerning significance, but for these purposes, make a judgment based on your honest impressions.)

2. Does this support the theory that the bisection of the line is critical to the illusion, and not some difference in judging vertical and horizontal lines? If it does support that theory, is the data conclusive?

3. Have you noticed any strengths or problems associated with the method of limits?

Measuring Illusions, continued
Simultaneous Contrast

Simultaneous brightness contrast occurs when a test stimulus' brightness is influenced by the brightness of its background. Typically, test stimuli that are presented surrounded by a very dark background look brighter than when they are presented on a brighter background. One theory of contrast is based on the concept of lateral inhibition. That is, the lateral inhibition affecting the test stimulus is greater for brighter backgrounds than for darker backgrounds. As inhibition increases, the perceived brightness of the test stimulus decreases. If lateral inhibition is important, then the size of the test stimulus should influence the magnitude of the contrast effect. Smaller stimuli might be expected to show a greater contrast effect than larger stimuli. This experiment will allow you to manipulate test stimulus size and evaluate this theory.

Collect data for each of the test sizes. Your task is to decide whether the test circle on the right is brighter than the test circle on the left. Remember that the stimuli are presented briefly and that your response will not register unless the response buttons show bold type (highlighted). Save your data for each condition.

RESULTS & DISCUSSION

1. Report your data for each of the three stimulus sizes. Did the contrast effect change as stimulus size changed? (Ignore the fact that you have not performed any statistical tests. Give your general impression of the data.)

2. Does your data support the idea that lateral inhibition causes brightness contrast? Support your answer. Is any other data needed to be sure?

3. What is a PSE? How is it obtained using the method of limits? How could you find the difference threshold using your raw data?

DL by the Method of Limits

The difference threshold (or DL; *L* refers to limen, a term for threshold) represents the smallest difference between two stimuli that can be detected. When the method of limits is used to measure the DL, two stimuli are presented on each trial. One is held constant, and the other is varied along some dimension (size, intensity, weight, etc.). As characteristic of the method of limits, the magnitude of the difference is varied in equal, orderly steps in ascending and descending series. The observer responds as to whether the comparison stimulus is greater than (larger, brighter, heavier, etc.), equal to, or less than (smaller, less bright, lighter, etc.) the constant stimulus.

In this activity, two triangles will be presented on each trial. Respond whether triangle B looks smaller than, bigger than, or equal in size to triangle A. Because three types of responses are allowed, there will be two response crossover points for each series. Pay attention to the computation of each of these crossovers and how they are used to compute the DL.

RESULTS & DISCUSSION

1. Report your results, showing all three measurements for each series, in addition to the final means.

2. What does the upper difference threshold represent? What does the lower difference threshold represent? How do these relate to the DL?

3. What is the point of subjective equality and how is it computed?

4. Did you ever answer EQUAL twice in a row? If so, no computations were done for that series because of the way this program is designed. When do you think more than one EQUAL response would be likely to occur in a real experiment, and what does it mean (assuming the person wasn't told to respond EQUAL only once)? Could a DL be obtained even if this happens? Explain why or why not?

Just Noticeable Difference

Although your text uses the term DL to refer to the difference threshold, you sometimes will see the term "just noticeable difference" used in other sources. Just noticeable difference (JND) describes what a difference threshold really is – the smallest difference that may be detected. Although the JND may provide useful information about a sensory system's acuity, the concept had greater significance in the early research on psychophysics. Fechner proposed that the JND could be used as a unit of perceived magnitude. That is, he assumed a difference of one JND represents the same difference in perceived magnitude, no matter what the actual magnitude of the two stimuli might be.

This exercise requires you to adjust stimuli until they are "just noticeably different." As indicated in the exercise, this is not the typical method used to measure JND. Here, the two stimuli are initially set significantly different in one characteristic (area, length, or saturation), and you have to reduce that difference until it is just detectable. Be sure to note how the JNDs obtained for the different stimulus characteristics compare.

RESULTS & DISCUSSION

1. Report the JND obtained for each task.

2. Compare the JND for each task. What does this tell us about our ability to perceive area, length, and saturation.

Weber's Law and Weber Fraction

When Weber obtained measurements of the JND (DL) for stimuli of many different weights, he found that the JND was not the same for all weights. Heavier weights did not yield the same JND as lighter weights. This relationship was not random, however. Weber found that the JND was constant if represented as a proportion of the standard stimulus, a "Weber fraction." This relationship is represented in Weber' Law, the subject of this exercise.

Click on each weight to plot JND/standard weight for each standard weight. Be sure to note the characteristics of the resulting psychophysical function. Weber's Law predicts a function with 0 slope (flat line).

RESULTS & DISCUSSION

1. Reproduce the psychophysical function plotted in this exercise. What can be concluded from this function?

2. How is Weber's Law usually stated? What does each of the terms represent?

3. According to this exercise, what is the Weber fraction for weight? If the Weber fraction for judgments of pressure is approximately 0.14, are people more sensitive to differences in weight or pressure? Why do you come to this conclusion?

DL vs. Weight

As should be clear by now, your perception does not necessarily precisely match the physical characteristics of a stimulus. You do not necessarily see two stimuli as the same size, even if they are equal. Although perceptions might not match the physical reality, there are predictable relationships between perception and the physical stimulus. Psychophysical functions represent the relationship between the perception of a stimulus and the physical attributes of that stimulus.

In this exercise you will see an example of a psychophysical function. The DL is plotted for several standard stimuli that differ in magnitude. Click on the weight to plot the DL for that weight. Note the characteristics of this psychophysical function.

RESULTS & DISCUSSION

1. Reproduce the psychophysical function.

2. What does the nature of the function tell us about the relationship between DL and stimulus magnitude?

Scaling Vision

Psychophysics studies the relationship between the physical stimulus and perception. One major issue in psychophysics concerns how changes in the stimulus are related to changes in perception. Wundt found that the relationship between physical changes and perceptual ones was not a linear one. However, changes of equal proportion generally produced equal changes in perception. Fechner described a slightly different relationship, and in more recent times, Stevens added his own conclusions.

This experiment uses Stevens' magnitude estimation technique to examine how the visual system responds to three different stimulus dimensions. In this procedure a standard stimulus is assigned a standard value, and the observer provides a rating for a new stimulus in relation to that standard. By examining the ratings to the new stimuli, the relationship between the physical and the perceptual may be established. Be sure to read the instructions for the experiment carefully and practice before beginning.

As you complete this exercise, you should try to answer several questions: (1) Do the three stimulus dimensions produce the same type of function? (2) Does the range of stimuli used to establish the scaling function matter? (3) Does the magnitude of the standard influence the results? To answer these questions you will need to gather data for several different situations. Manipulate the parameters as needed, and be sure to print out (and save) your data each time.

RESULTS & DISCUSSION

1. Present your data for the three different stimulus dimensions. What type of function did each produce? What does this tell us about the psychophysical relationship for each of these dimensions?

2. Did the range of stimuli tested effect the nature of the psychophysical functions you obtained? Present data to support your conclusion. What does this suggest?

3. Did the magnitude of the standard influence the results? Present data to support your conclusion. Why might this be important?

Response Compression and Expansion

Fechner's Law proposed that perceived magnitude is proportional to the log of stimulus magnitude, with the proportion for a particular sensory task being a constant. This is expressed as $S = c(\log I)$, where S is the sensation, I is the physical intensity of the stimulus, and c is a constant of proportionality that is related to the Weber fraction. More recently, however, Stevens proposed a psychophysical function based on magnitude estimation data that has proven to be more accurate than Fechner's Law.

Stevens' Power Law is expressed as $P = KS^n$, where P is the perceived magnitude, S is the stimulus intensity raised to the power n, and K is a constant. Each sensory modality has its own exponent n, and this exponent reflects how changes in physical intensity relate to changes in perception. Some values of the exponent lead to response expansion, an increase in perceptual magnitude that is actually greater than the increase in the physical stimulus. Other values lead to response compression, increases in perceptual magnitude that are smaller than the increase in the physical stimulus.

This exercise illustrates response compression and expansion by plotting the functions for different exponents. Note the exponents for each of the functions.

RESULTS & DISCUSSION

1. Describe the shape of the function in which $n > 1.0$. Repeat for $n = 1.0$ and for $n < 1.0$. Which function represents response compression? Response expansion? Response linearity?

2. Describe a real-world situation in which a sensory system with a high exponent would be more useful than one with a low exponent. Why would this be true?

Chapter 2: Introduction to the Physiology of Perception

Virtual Labs for Chapter 2:

Cortical Areas
3D Virtual Brain
Structure of Neuron
Oscilloscopes and Intracellular Recording
Resting Potential
Phases of Action Potential
Nerve Impulse Coding and Stimulus Strength
Synaptic Transmission
Lock and Key Neurotransmitter Action
Excitation and Inhibition
The Human Eye
Cross Section of the Retina
Anatomy of the Eye
Visual Path Within the Eyeball
Mapping the Blind Spot
Filling in the Blind Spot
Dark Adaptation of the Rods and Cones
Types of Cones

Cortical Areas

Although information for a specific sense eventually might be transmitted to many different brain areas via a very complex neural pathway, each sense has a primary reception area in the cortex. The primary reception area is the first cortical area where input from a sensory organ is received and processed. Processing in the primary reception area is often described as "basic" with "complex" processes occurring at "higher" brain areas. For example, the primary reception area for vision appears to process very basic aspects of patterns – spots, lines, contrast – whereas the more complex processing resulting in the perception of complete objects or forms is completed elsewhere.

In this exercise different senses will be linked to the brain areas containing their respective primary receptive area. Click on the different SIGNAL buttons to highlight a specific sensory area. Note the cortical area and sense identified in the boxes below the diagram of the brain.

RESULTS & DISCUSSION

1. Identify the senses included in this exercise, and give the cortical areas associated with each.

2. The doctrine of specific nerve energies states that sensory quality (visual vs. auditory vs. olfactory, etc.) is determined by which neurons are stimulated and carry neural input to the brain. Of what relevance is the current exercise to the basic idea of the doctrine of specific nerve energies?

3D Virtual Brain

Although perception involves processing in multiple areas of the brain, each brain area is associated with certain specific functions. Sensory information for each sense, for example, is transmitted initially to different regions of the brain. Even within a sensory system, different types of processing are carried out by different brain areas.

In this exercise you will examine the different brain structures, and you will learn the functions of each structure. The model of the brain may be rotated, enlarged, and dissected so that internal structures are visible. By positioning the cursor over a brain area, the name of the structure and the functions associated with that area will be displayed.

Begin with the brain oriented so that the front of the brain (the blue section) is on the right and you are viewing the brain from the side. Note the name of each structure and its major functions. Pay special attention to areas associated with sensation and perception. Rotate the brain so that you can see the entire 3D representation. Finally, use the DISSECT controls to remove the cerebral hemisphere and reveal the subcortical structures. Note the name and function of each subcortical structure represented.

RESULTS AND DISCUSSION

1. For each lobe of the cerebral cortex (the purple, pink, blue, and yellow regions), describe its location and identify its major function. Identify the brain areas associated with the sensory sytems.

2. Where are the cerebellum, pons, and medulla located, and what major functions are associated with each of these structures?

3. Which structures are located deep within the brain? Identify the major functions associated with each structure. Which structure plays an important role in processing sensory input? Where is it located?

Structure of Neuron

Psychophysical studies examine the relationship between the physical stimulus and the ultimate perceptual effect. This approach can give us important information, but it deals with only the beginning and end points of a very complex sequence of events. It does not directly consider the neural activity created by the environmental stimulation, nor the way in which that neural activity is processed and represents the nature of the stimulation. Fully understanding the process of perception requires consideration of the physiological activity that produces it.

In this exercise, the different parts of a neuron are presented, and the process of neural firing is shown. Click on the name for each part of the neuron, and see the corresponding areas in the diagram highlighted. Pay attention to the information provided about each part. Although the basic components are characteristic of neurons in general, note that not all neurons are exactly alike. Find some of those differences when you view the diagram of the sensory neuron.

RESULTS & DISCUSSION

1. Where is the axon hillock, and what is its significance?

2. How does the neuron in the first diagram differ from the sensory neuron shown in the second diagram? Identify one other way in which neurons may differ, depending on their function and location in the nervous system.

Oscilloscopes and Intracellular Recording

An oscilloscope is a machine that measures electrical input and displays that electrical activity in a visual form on a screen. It shows not only the voltage of the input, but also how that voltage changes over time. Oscilloscopes, therefore, can be very useful for providing a visual representation of neural activity.

In this exercise you will get a basic demonstration of how an oscilloscope represents the electrical potential of a neuron and how that potential changes when the neuron is stimulated. To see how the oscilloscope represents different voltages, move the cursor to the left and to the right, and notice how the line on the oscilloscope screen changes as voltage is manipulated. The flat line indicates that the voltage is constant across time.

After you understand how changes in voltage look on the oscilloscope, click on RESET, the click on INSERT MICROELECTRODE to insert the electrode into the neuron. Note the function shown on the oscilloscope. What you are seeing now is a representation of the resting potential of the neuron, the electrical potential of the neuron when there is no stimulation. Next, click on the ON-OFF switch, and note how the function changes. Finally, click on NEURAL TISSUE to see how neural tissue looks with a microelectrode in place.

RESULTS & DISCUSSION

1. How did the function on the oscilloscope change when you changed the voltage from 0 mV to 50 mV?

2. When you inserted the electrode into the neuron, at what voltage was the electrical activity?

3. What happened when you clicked the ON-OFF switch? Why did this happen?

Resting Potential

When a neuron is not receiving input from a receptor or other neuron, it has a resting potential of approximately -70 millivolts. This demonstration explains the cause of the resting potential. Pay special attention to the conditions inside and outside of the cell, and note how these conditions relate to the resting potential.

RESULTS & DISCUSSION

1. Identify the three substances that are featured in this description of the resting potential. Where is each substance located?

2. Why is the charge inside the neuron more negative than the charge outside the neuron?

3. When a neuron is stimulated and an action potential is generated, the charge of the neuron becomes more positive. Based on what you have learned in this demonstration, what chemical change do you think causes the cell's charge to become more positive?

Phases of Action Potential

When a neuron is at rest, sodium ions (Na^+) and potassium ions (K^+) are unevenly distributed inside and outside the neuron, and the inside of the neuron is negatively charged relative to the extracellular fluid. An action potential, or neural impulse, is generated when stimulation causes the membrane of the neuron to change in permeability to sodium ions (Na^+) and potassium ions (K^+), allowing sodium and potassium ions to move into and out of the cell, respectively, thus changing the charge of the neuron in that region.

The process that leads to the formation of an action potential is simulated and described in this exercise. Move the cursor along the function on the oscilloscope, and note what happens in the diagram of the neuron to the right. An explanation of what is occurring is shown at the top of the screen. Be sure you understand how the movement of ions is reflected in the function shown on the oscilloscope.

RESULTS & DISCUSSION

1. What causes the inside of the neuron to become more positively charged relative to the extracellular fluid? Why does the charge then become more negative, and eventually hyperpolarized?

2. What is the sodium-potassium pump, and what role does it play?

Nerve Impulse Coding and Stimulus Strength

One important issue in the study of sensation and perception is how stimulus characteristics are represented in the nervous system. In the mid-1800s, Johannes Mueller proposed the doctrine of specific nerve energies to explain how different types of perceptions (e.g., visual versus auditory) are determined. This doctrine explained that the specific nerves that carry the information determine the nature of the resulting perception. In other words, if the input comes via nerves from the eye, we see, whereas if the input comes from neurons from the ear, we hear.

Although that basic idea has some merit for differentiating between senses, it does not address the issue of how differences within a sense are represented. For example, how can changes in intensity be represented? How is the information from the neurons different for a weak stimulus than for a strong stimulus? The information available in the nervous system consists of action potentials, the activation of neurons. How can the action potential be used to represent different stimulus qualities and quantities?

This exercise illustrates how neural activity varies when the intensity of stimulation is varied. Remember that each "spike" on the oscilloscope screen is just a compressed view of an action potential. Click on the different stimulus conditions, and note how the neural activity changes as stimulation changes.

RESULTS & DISCUSSION

1. How did changes in stimulus intensity affect the neural activity? Did stronger stimulation produce a stronger (taller) action potential?

2. How did the neural activity resulting from very intense stimulation differ from that for moderate stimulation? What does this suggest?

3. What happened to neural activity when there was no stimulation? What does this imply?

Synaptic Transmission

The action potential is the result of an exchange of ions in and out of the neuron that occurs when the permeability of the cell membrane changes. What happens when the end of the neuron is reached? Neurons are not in direct contact with each other; there is a space between them. So how can the action potential cross the gap, the synapse, and initiate an action potential in the next neuron?

This exercise illustrates how an action potential moves along two neurons. It introduces the terms presynaptic and postsynaptic, and illustrates the activity at the synapse that allows different neurons to communicate. Be sure to click on the highlighted, flashing box at the synapse to see what activity occurs at the synapse.

RESULTS & DISCUSSION

1. Define presynaptic neuron and postsynaptic neuron.

2. How is information transmitted across the synapse?

3. What are the possible responses of the postsynaptic neuron following the release of neurotransmitters?

Lock and Key Neurotransmitter Action

The "lock and key" concept has been proposed to explain why different substances in the synapse have different effects on the postsynaptic membrane. According to this concept, the receptors in the postsynaptic membrane may be compared to a lock on a door. Only keys with a specific shape, matching that of the lock's internal mechanism, will turn and free the lock.

This exercise illustrates the lock and key concept applied to neurotransmitter action. Note how the two classes of substances compare in terms of shape, and what happens when they contact the receptors.

RESULTS & DISCUSSION

1. How does the lock and key concept relate to neurotransmitters and postsynaptic receptors?

2. What happens if a chemical is similar to a neurotransmitter, but doesn't perfectly match the receptor?

Excitation and Inhibition

When neural transmission is discussed, it is common to think that when an action potential reaches the end of the neuron and causes the release of neurotransmitters, the effect will be the excitation of the postsynaptic neuron. However, the effect of the input can be either excitatory or inhibitory. Activity in one neuron can inhibit activity in another.

Each neuron synapses with many other neurons. Some of these other neurons may have an inhibitory effect, and others may have an excitatory effect. This exercise illustrates the effect of excitatory and inhibitory input and what happens when a combination of both is present.

Click on the different numbers associated with each type of input to change the strength of that input (or perhaps the number of presynaptic neurons providing that type of input). Be sure to test each level and note its effect on the neural activity. Also, test combinations of excitatory and inhibitory input and note the effect.

RESULTS & DISCUSSION

1. How did postsynaptic neural activity change as a function of the strength of excitatory and inhibitory input? When was neural activity greatest? When was neural activity effectively zero?

2. What general rule might be proposed to describe how the postsynaptic neuron responds to input from multiple neurons?

3. Neurons have a baseline firing rate that is maintained even when no stimulus is present. Why is this so important or useful?

The Human Eye

Each of the major parts of the human eye plays an important role in vision. Like a camera, the condition and arrangement of the component parts will determine the quality of the picture created. A poor quality lens produces a poor picture. The type of film may impact picture quality, too. Understanding the structural characteristics of the eye and the way each structure functions will be important for understanding many aspects of vision.

This exercise will let you practice labeling the major structures of the human eye. After studying the related material in your text, drag and drop the name of each structure to its appropriate location. If you are wrong, your answer won't stick.

RESULTS & DISCUSSION

1. Identify the major parts of the eye included in this exercise. Which one is the rather large, light green structure inside the eye? What is its function?

2. Where is the optic nerve located? What is the relationship between it and the blind spot?

3. The fovea is a specific location in which eye structure?

Cross Section of the Retina

The visual receptors and their associated neurons are located in the retina of the eye. Their arrangement and characteristics are important factors that influence visual perception. As you will see in this cross-section of the retina, there are several different types of cells located in the retina. Each one has a particular relationship to the others and its own function in transmitting visual input.

One interesting thing that is not indicated in this diagram is the relationship of the retinal structures to the incoming light. Although common sense might suggest that the receptor cells should be pointing toward the incoming light, in reality, they are deep in the retina and point toward the back of the eye, away from the incoming light. The light has to penetrate through the outer layers of cells before reaching the receptors, and yet we still see clearly.

Drag and drop each label into its appropriate place in the diagram. If you are wrong, your answer won't stick.

RESULTS & DISCUSSION

1. Identify the five types of cells shown in the cross-section of the retina. Describe their positions.

2. The receptor cells have three different segments. Name the three segments and identify which segment contains the photosensitive pigment.

3. Which cells transmit information from the receptors toward the optic nerve, and which transmit information laterally (side to side)?

Anatomy of the Eye

Light strikes an object in the environment and is reflected. The light enters the eye, passing through several structures, and is focused on the back surface of the eye. This demonstration reveals the major structures of the eye and illustrates how an image of an object in the environment is formed. Note how the image in the eye relates to the object in the environment.

The model of the eye may be rotated by placing the "hand" on the eye and dragging the eye in one direction or another. Rotate the eye so that you can see all seven major structures portrayed here. After you have identified all structures, move the hand off the eye and to the left edge of the picture. A tree should appear, and the tree's image will move through the eye.

RESULTS & DISCUSSION

1. Identify the seven major structures and describe their locations.

2. Describe the path light travels as it enters and moves through the eye. What is the last structure it encounters?

3. What is meant by distal stimulus and proximal stimulus?

4. How does the tree's image on the retina differ from the image as it enters the eye?

Visual Path Within the Eyeball

This segment illustrates the path visual input follows through the different structures of the retina. Note that the light must pass through several layers of cells before it contacts the receptors. Pay special attention to the number of receptors associated with each bipolar cell, and the number of bipolar cells associated with each ganglion cell. This will be very important information during the discussion of acuity and sensitivity. Also, don't miss the information about the optic nerve.

RESULTS & DISCUSSION

1. Trace the pathway from receptor to optic nerve.

2. What kind of cells make up the optic nerve?

3. Does each ganglion cell carry information from a single receptor cell? How might the number of receptors associated with a ganglion cell be important in influencing what is seen?

Mapping the Blind Spot

All the neurons in the retina converge at one location to leave the eyeball and form the optic nerve. This region of the retina contains no rods or cones, creating a blind spot in each eye. Under normal circumstances people are not usually aware of this gap in vision, partly because the same region of the visual field is not associated with the blind spot in both eyes.

In this exercise you will create a map of your right eye's blind spot. Full instructions are included in the exercise, but two things are essential: You must not move your head during the experiment, and you must keep your focus on the fixation point when deciding whether you can see the test stimulus. Moving your head or fixation point will shift the location of the blind spot relative to the screen, and this will distort the map you create.

When you have completed the exercise, the locations in which you did not see the test stimulus will be shown. The retinal images of stimuli that occur in those visual field locations fall within the blind spot. Note the size, shape, and location of the area corresponding to your blind spot.

RESULTS & DISCUSSION

1. Describe the location, size, and shape of your blind spot.

2. Given what you know about the geometry of the relationship a stimulus' position in the visual field and its image's position on the retina, describe where the blind spot is located in the retina (e.g., Above or below the fovea? Nasal side or in the lateral periphery?)

3. Some people don't see the stimulus when it is presented in the most distant display locations. What does this represent?

Filling in the Blind Spot

As you have learned, there is a region in each retina called the blind spot. This region contains no photoreceptive cells, so it sends no visual input to the brain. Even though this region is of significant size, you do not perceive a gap in your vision under normal circumstances. One reason for this is that the information that falls within the blind spot of one eye will not fall within the blind spot of the other eye. However, the blind spot is not normally noticed even when only one eye is open, so something else is involved in preventing awareness of the blind spot.

In this demonstration you will observe a phenomenon usually called "filling in" the blind spot. The instructions with this demonstration do not indicate you should close one eye, but the effect will be stronger if you view the stimulus with only your right eye. Be sure to look steadily at the fixation point, but note what happens to the blank circular region to the right side. Restart the demonstration, but this time look directly at the blank circular region, rather than the fixation point.

RESULTS & DISCUSSION

1. Describe what you observed. Did the circular area change when you kept your fixation on the small dot? Did you observe the same change when you looked directly at the circular area?

2. Based on what you observed, why is the blind spot not usually noticed?

3. Why might this be considered an adaptive, positive attribute of the perceptual system?

Dark Adaptation of the Rods and Cones

Most people have had the experience of walking from a bright environment into a very dark one and finding they could see almost nothing at first. However, after spending a few minutes in the dark, people notice that things that originally were not visible at all have become quite obvious. This change in sensitivity is dramatic and very adaptive.

The state of the receptors is of vital importance to the sensitivity of the visual system. The amount and the nature of the photosensitive pigments in the receptors is a primary determinant of how intense a stimulus must be in order to be detected. Exposure to light reduces the system's sensitivity (increases the absolute threshold), and maximum sensitivity is regained only when the photopigments have fully regenerated.

This exercise illustrates the changes in sensitivity that occur during a period in the dark as receptors undergo dark adaptation. The dark adaptation curve that is generated is a plot of the absolute threshold over time. Pay special attention to the unique shape and timing of the functions for the cones only, rods only, and both receptors combined.

Note that experiments 1, 2, and 3 mentioned in this exercise refer to the experiments in which dark adaptation curves for rods and cones combined, cones only, and rods only described in your text.

RESULTS & DISCUSSION

1. How do the functions obtained for cones only and rods only compare?

2. Why is there a "break" in the dark adaptation curve obtained for rods and cones combined?

3. Describe a real-world situation in which dark adaptation occurs and impacts perception and behavior.

Types of Cones

The receptor cells for vision are the rods and cones. Cones differ from rods in several ways, including structural characteristics, distribution on the retina, the degree of convergence with ganglion cells, and the photosensitive pigments they contain. The difference in photosensitive pigments leads to perhaps the most significant difference in the function of rods and cones: Only cones permit color perception.

As you will see, each cone contains one of three types of photopigments, and these photopigments are not the same as that found in rods. Each type of photopigment responds to a range of wavelengths of light, but these ranges differ as a function of the type of photopigment involved. Also, each photopigment reacts maximally to a different wavelength of light, leading to a designation as "short wavelength," "middle wavelength," or "long wavelength" cones or photopigments. In the discussion of color vision you will learn that the presence of three different kinds of photopigments is critical to the richness of our color perception.

Plotting a cone's reaction to different wavelengths of light produces the cone's spectral sensitivity curve. In this exercise you will see the range of wavelengths to which each type of cone photopigment responds, and the spectral sensitivity curve will be plotted. Click on a cone to see that cone's characteristics. Clicking on the cone with mixed colors will plot all three spectral sensitivity curves in the same graph. Pay attention to the range of each curve and the wavelength to which sensitivity is greatest.

RESULTS & DISCUSSION

1. Describe the spectral sensitivity curves for each type of cone, and identify the wavelengths to which each cone is maximally sensitive.

2. Do the different cones respond to a narrow or broad range of wavelengths?

3. Describe how each type of cone would respond to a 500 nm wavelength light.

Chapter 3: Neurons and Perception

Virtual Labs for Chapter 3:

Cross Section of the Retina
Receptor Wiring and Sensitivity
Receptor Wiring and Acuity
Lateral Inhibition
Hermann Grid
Lateral Inhibition in the Hermann Grid
Mach Bands
Intensity and Brightness
Inhibition and Mach Band
Simultaneous Contrast
Simultaneous Contrast: Static
Simultaneous Contrast: Dynamic
Simple Neural Circuits
Mapping Receptive Fields
Receptive Field Mapping
Stimulus Size and Receptive Fields
Receptive Fields and Stimulus Size and Shape
The Visual Pathways
Simple Cells in the Cortex
Complex Cells in the Cortex
Calculating Grating Contrast
Contrast Sensitivity
Orientation Aftereffect
Size Aftereffect
Spatial Vision

Cross Section of the Retina

The visual receptors and their associated neurons are located in the retina of the eye. Their arrangement and characteristics are important factors that influence visual perception. As you will see in this cross-section of the retina, there are several different types of cells located in the retina. Each one has a particular relationship to the others and its own function in transmitting visual input.

One interesting thing that is not indicated in this diagram is the relationship of the retinal structures to the incoming light. Although common sense might suggest that the receptor cells should be pointing toward the incoming light, in reality, they are deep in the retina and point toward the back of the eye, away from the incoming light. The light has to penetrate through the outer layers of cells before reaching the receptors, and yet we still see clearly.

Drag and drop each label into its appropriate place in the diagram. If you are wrong, your answer won't stick.

RESULTS & DISCUSSION

1. Identify the five types of cells shown in the cross-section of the retina. Describe their positions.

2. The receptor cells have three different segments. Name the three segments and identify which segment contains the photosensitive pigment.

3. Which cells transmit information from the receptors toward the optic nerve, and which transmit information laterally (side to side)?

Receptor Wiring and Sensitivity

One of the differences between rods and cones is that rods operate at much lower levels of light than cones operate. That is, rods will respond to much weaker stimuli than cones will in a dark environment. Although the difference in the pigments found in rods and cones is partly responsible, it does not account for the entire difference in perceptual sensitivity. Another very important factor is the relationship between the receptors and the ganglion cells.

This exercise illustrates the physical relationship between the ganglion cells and the rods and cones and demonstrates the impact this arrangement has on sensitivity. Click on the lights to illuminate one type of receptor. Click on the numbers under INTENSITY to vary the intensity of the illumination. Note whether a flashing green spot appears on the ganglion cell's axon, signifying a neural response. Note that the rate of flashing relates to the frequency of the neural response. Note also what level of stimulation at the ganglion level is required for a response to occur, and what must occur for this level to be reached. Repeat for the other receptor. An explanation is available in text or audio format.

RESULTS & DISCUSSION

1. What illumination level was required for a ganglion cell in the rod system to respond? For a ganglion cell in the cone system?

2. Compare the relationship of rods to ganglion cells with the relationship of cones to ganglion cells. How can this explain why rod-based vision is more sensitive than cone-based vision?

3. Astronomers have known for centuries that stars that are visible in the periphery (to the side) of one's field of vision sometimes can no longer be seen when viewed directly. Explain why this occurs, using what you have learned in this exercise. (Hint: Think about where rods and cones are located.)

Receptor Wiring and Acuity

One of the major differences between rods and cones is that cones allow much better acuity than do rods. For example, you might have noticed that you can easily read a word in very small print when you look directly at it, but that you struggle to see it clearly if it is in the periphery (to the side) of your field of vision. This occurs because when you look directly at a word, its image falls in the fovea, a location in the retina that has only cones, but when a word is in the periphery, its image falls on a retinal area with mostly rods. The difference in the rod and cone photopigments cannot explain this, so what can?

As with differences in sensitivity, the answer involves the neural relationship between the receptors and the ganglion cells. This exercise illustrates this relationship and how it affects acuity.

Begin by noting how the rods and cones are linked to the ganglion cells. Click on the far left light above the rods, and then click on the adjacent light. Both lights will remain on, stimulating two different rods. Repeat with the other lights. For each pair of lights, note whether the information at the level of the ganglion cells indicates that two points of stimulation are perceived, rather than just one. Repeat this procedure with the cones. For an explanation, click on either the SCRIPT or AUDIO buttons.

RESULTS & DISCUSSION

1. For each type of receptor, identify which two lights had to be illuminated in order to create a perception of two separate points of light. How far apart did the two lights have to be?

2. How can the neural wiring of receptors to ganglion cells account for the difference in acuity that occurs when rods are involved as compared to when cones are involved?

3. If your back is lightly touched by the tines of a fork, you probably will feel a continuous, line-like pattern of pressure. If your cheek is similarly touched, you probably will feel each of the four tines individually. Given what you've learned in this exercise, what do you predict might account for the difference in perception at different places on the body?

Lateral Inhibition

Neural circuits and receptive fields clearly demonstrate that a neuron's activity level is influenced by the total input it receives. Inhibitory input may offset some or all of the effect of excitatory input. In many circumstances the inhibitory and excitatory input comes from neurons at "earlier" levels of a neural circuit or pathway. However, neurons may be influenced by other neurons at essentially the same level of the neural pathway. Such a situation exists for the effect known as lateral inhibition.

In lateral inhibition, a neuron's activity is influenced by the level of activity in adjacent neurons. Specifically, the response of the neuron associated with one receptor will be inhibited when an adjacent receptor is stimulated and produces activity in an adjacent neuron. Lateral (side-to-side) connections between neurons allow this type of interaction.

In this exercise, lateral inhibition is simulated. Note how the response of the neuron changes when each light is turned on, and pay attention to the influence that Light B's intensity has on the firing rate.

RESULTS & DISCUSSION

1. How did the firing rate change when Light A was turned on? What happened when Light B was turned on and stimulated nearby receptors?

2. How does stimulus intensity relate to lateral inhibition?

3. The lateral plexus is responsible for lateral inhibition in the visual system of the horseshoe crab. The human eye does not have a lateral plexus, but lateral inhibition occurs. What structures in the human retina allow lateral influences on neural activity? (Hint: Look at a diagram of the human retina.)

Hermann Grid

The basic Hermann (or Hermann-Hering) grid, which dates back to the 1800s, consists of a grid of intersecting white lines on a black background. Darker, shadowy areas are perceived in the intersections, rather than the white of which the grid is actually constructed. The version of the illusion shown in this demonstration, however, is an even more remarkable one. It is known as the scintillating Hermann grid and was first reported by Lengelbach in the late 20th century. In this version, the grid itself is grey on a black background, and white circles are placed in the intersections. The white circles in the region near fixation look white, but the circles in the periphery are perceived to have a dark circle inside them. Eye movements cause a flickering, or scintillating effect.

This demonstration will allow you to experience the scintillating Hermann grid illusion. Do not stare at the grid. Move your eyes freely over the figure. Compare the appearance of the intersections near fixation and in the periphery. Also, try viewing the figure at a 45° angle. Some researchers have reported changes in the illusion when viewed in that manner.

RESULTS & DISCUSSION

1. Report what you perceived when you viewed the figure in the normal orientation. Did you experience a scintillating effect? Did the intersections near fixation look the same as those in the periphery?

2. The standard Hermann-Hering grid is typically explained in terms of lateral inhibition. Can lateral inhibition account for this version of the illusion, including the difference between what is seen near fixation and in the periphery? Explain.

3. Report what you perceived when you viewed the figure at an angle. Was the illusion the same? How does this effect the usual explanation of the illusion?

Lateral Inhibition in the Hermann Grid

The Hermann Grid is a white grid on a black background. Although the white lines in the grid are equally bright or white, people see them as darker or shadowed in the intersections. This illusion is quite strong, and awareness that it is an illusion has no impact on perception. Like other illusions, this demonstrates that the stimulus energy that comes into contact with the receptors is only one factor that determines the observer's perception. Perception is the result of not only the characteristics of the stimulus, but also may be influenced significantly by the nature of the nervous system and cognitive factors. In the case of the Hermann Grid, the illusion is caused by the neural circuitry of the nervous system and receptors.

This demonstration illustrates how lateral inhibition can explain the Hermann Grid illusion. Pay special attention to the spatial location of the receptor cells relative to the grid and how activity in each cell impacts the output of Cell A or Cell B. Compare the final activity level of Cell A and Cell B when all of the other cells are being stimulated.

RESULTS & DISCUSSION

1. Report the activity level of Cell A under the following conditions: (a) Cell A is stimulated; (b) Cell A and Cell L are stimulated; (c) Cell A, Cell L, and Cell R are stimulated; (d) all cells are stimulated. Repeat, substituting Cell B for Cell A.

2. Why does Cell L inhibit Cell A more than Cell L inhibits Cell B?

3. Why does the Hermann Grid illusion occur?

Mach Bands

Mach bands are illusory bands of different lightness that appear on either side of a lightness boundary. On the darker side of the boundary, the Mach band is an even darker strip. On the lighter side of the boundary, the Mach band is an even lighter strip. Mach bands are the result of inhibitory processes in the retina. When one neuron is active, it inhibits activity in nearby neurons. Neurons with receptive fields in the middle of an area are all equally inhibited by neighboring neurons, and thus, the lightness of the area is even. However, neurons with receptive fields near the boundary will be inhibited more than their neighbors toward the middle because of the adjacent lighter region, and this leads to the perception of a darker band. When the adjacent area is darker, inhibition is reduced, and the result is the perception of a lighter band.

This demonstration offers the opportunity to see the effects of lateral inhibition and the response patterns that lead to the perception of Mach bands. You should draw a lightness profile, and then click on CALCULATE to plot the response function. SHOW FUNCTION produces a representation of the spread of the inhibition. Adjust the parameters that vary the spread of inhibition and the general activity level of the cells, and see how this influences the response function. Pay attention to how increasing amplitude changes the response profile at different levels of lightness. Also, compare the response profiles and evidence of Mach bands for lightness profiles with sharp contours and for those with more gradual contours.

RESULTS & DISCUSSION

1. Compare the response profiles and appearance of Mach bands associated with lightness profiles with sharp contours and with more gradual contours. Why do they differ?

2. How did changing the amplitude of inhibition change the response profiles? Did the lightness of the area influence the impact of changes in amplitude? Explain.

3. When the spread of inhibition was adjusted, what happened?

Intensity and Brightness

In the study of sensation and perception, brightness and intensity do not mean exactly the same thing. Intensity is a purely physical characteristic. Brightness is a perceptual characteristic. Brightness certainly is related to intensity, of course. In general, as intensity increases, so too does brightness, but brightness sometimes does not reliably correspond to stimulus intensity. For example, in the Hermann Grid illusion some physically identical areas are perceived to be different. This is also true for another perceptual phenomenon known as Mach bands, thin bands in a stimulus that appear lighter or darker than the rest of the physically identical area.

This exercise maps the physical intensity measurements for a typical Mach band stimulus and contrasts those with the perception of stimulus brightness. Click on the INTENSITY button and drag the curser across the stimulus display to map the physical intensity. Repeat for BRIGHTNESS. Note how the two functions differ.

RESULTS & DISCUSSION

1. How does intensity change across the stimulus? Does the brightness function look the same? Compare the two functions.

2. Where in the stimulus do the differences occur?

Inhibition and Mach Band

When two adjacent areas differ in intensity, perhaps one being a light grey and one a darker grey, a thin band is perceived on each side of the border between the two areas. These are Mach bands. The band on the darker side looks even darker than the dark grey area, and the band on the lighter side looks even lighter than the light grey area. This occurs even though there is no physical difference between the region near the border and the region farther away. This illusion illustrates the fact that perception does not always reproduce the physical stimulus completely accurately.

This exercise presents a standard Mach band stimulus and demonstrates how the concept of neural receptive fields might provide an explanation for the illusion. Note the Mach bands that are clearly visible in the first stimulus. Click on the stimulus to separate the panels and see whether the Mach bands remain. Proceed to the neural explanation page and click on each receptive field to display the output of the associate neurons. Make sure you understand why the output differs in each case.

RESULTS & DISCUSSION

1. What happened when the stimulus array was separated? Did the Mach bands remain the same?

2. Describe the receptive fields shown in the simulation and compare their outputs. Why did their outputs differ?

3. How might receptive fields account for the Mach bands?

Simultaneous Contrast

Simultaneous contrast is a type of context effect. When two physically identical small figures are placed on backgrounds that differ significantly in intensity (e.g., one is white, the other dark grey), the two internal figures will be judged unequal in brightness or lightness. This phenomenon is known as simultaneous brightness contrast. A related phenomenon is simultaneous color contrast, in which the color of an internal figure is influenced by the color of its background. In all cases, the internal stimuli are physically identical, but they are not perceptually identical.

This exercise examines simultaneous brightness contrast. Begin by plotting the actual intensity of the stimulus, and then plot the brightness. See if the brightness plot reflects what you see. Note how the two functions compare, paying particular attention to the regions representing the inner square. Next, change the intensity of the background in the right-hand figure by adjusting the vertical control. Note how the brightness of the inner square changes, even though only the background is being manipulated.

RESULTS & DISCUSSION

1. Describe the appearance of the inner squares in the initial stimulus. How did this compare to their physical characteristics?

2. As the background was varied, how did your perception of the inner square vary? When did the inner square look brighter than the constant (left) inner square? When did it look darker? What is the general principle that describes simultaneous brightness contrast?

3. Lateral inhibition or neural receptive fields have provided explanations for other brightness illusions. Would either of these concepts provide a possible explanation for simultaneous contrast? Explain your answer.

Simultaneous Contrast: Static

The appearance of a stimulus depends on not only its own characteristics, but also the background's characteristics. For example, stimuli that appear on a dark background tend to look lighter than when they appear on a light background. This variation of lightness in different contexts is known as lightness (or brightness) contrast. Some simultaneous contrast has been explained in terms of lateral inhibition. That is, activity in one neuron causes the inhibition of neurons adjacent to it. However, the standard concept of lateral inhibition in the retina cannot account for all simultaneous contrast phenomena.

This demonstration illustrates static (steady-state) simultaneous contrast. Compare the lightness of the central circle on the two different backgrounds. To prove to yourself that they are actually the same lightness, view the central circles through two small holes in a piece of paper so that the background is the same for both circles.

RESULTS & DISCUSSION

1. Report what you perceived in this demonstration.

2. Why isn't lateral inhibition an adequate explanation for this kind of contrast effect?

Simultaneous Contrast: Dynamic

The appearance of a stimulus depends on not only its own characteristics, but also the background's characteristics. For example, stimuli that appear on a dark background tend to look lighter than when they appear on a light background. This variation of lightness in different contexts is known as lightness (or brightness) contrast. Some simultaneous contrast has been explained in terms of lateral inhibition. That is, activity in one neuron causes the inhibition of neurons adjacent to it. However, the standard concept of lateral inhibition in the retina cannot account for all simultaneous contrast phenomena.

This demonstration illustrates dynamic (involving change) simultaneous contrast. Note the change in lightness of the central circle as the background changes. To prove that the circle does not really change in lightness, click on WHITE (OR BLACK) and view the circle on a uniform background.

RESULTS & DISCUSSION

1. Report what you perceived in this demonstration.

2. What factors other than lateral inhibition might account for contrast effects like this?

Simple Neural Circuits

A neural circuit is a collection of neurons connected by synapses. Some circuits are linear, and each cell links directly with one other cell. Other circuits involve convergence where several cells send input to one cell in common. Within these circuits some synapses may be excitatory and others may be inhibitory, so activity from one part of the circuit may actually inhibit the activity in the next cell. Depending on the specific way cells are linked and the nature of the synapses involved, a neural circuit may be designed so that its response is highly specific to particular types of stimuli. Such neural circuits have been proposed as explanations for how "detector cells" in the brain might operate as part of pattern perception.

In this exercise you will explore three different types of neural circuits that vary in how neurons are linked and the kinds of synapses that are included. Be sure to begin with light #1 and continue in numerical order. A graph of the neural response will be created. Note how the response differs for each circuit, and think about this being useful in pattern perception. Make sure you understand how the type of synapse influences the output and the type of stimulus that will produce the maximum response.

RESULTS & DISCUSSION

1. If a small spot of light stimulates the receptors associated with the second neural circuit (convergence only), will the final cell (Cell I) in the circuit respond differently than if a large spot of light is the stimulus? Why or why not? Is this also true for the third neural circuit (convergence with inhibition)? Why or why not?

2. This simulation always had a stimulus of increasing size. Think about how the circuit would respond if a stimulus varied in location instead. Describe the activity of Cell H that will occur if a small spot of light moved from left to right to stimulate Cells A through Cell G one after another in the second neural circuit (convergence only). Compare this to what would happen for the third (convergence and inhibition) neural circuit.

3. Which type of circuit will provide high sensitivity? Which type of circuit will provide high acuity?

Mapping Receptive Fields

When you look at a picture on your computer screen, the images that you see as whole figures are actually composed of many tiny, active pixels. A similar situation exists for the retina and the neural signal produced by a visual stimulus. The receptor cells are similar to the pixels on the computer screen, with each active receptor representing stimulation on a tiny point in the retina.

Because of the structure of the neural pathway, these individual signals do not remain individual all the way to the brain, however. Some neurons converge on another neuron in the circuit. That neuron's activity thus reflects stimulation of any of the receptors that input to the neuron.

To map a receptive field of a neuron, the physical area in which stimulation produces a response, points on the retina are stimulated systematically, and neural activity are monitored. Because of the potential complexity of the neural circuit linking receptors to a ganglion cell, a cell's output may differ based on the specific location stimulated in its receptive field.

In this exercise, you will map a typical receptive field for one ganglion cell. A small spot of light will move across the field, and any neural response that results will be noted. Be sure to pay attention to the changes in firing rate so that you understand how the different regions are identified. Note the shape of the receptive field and the type of response produced by stimulation in different regions.

RESULTS & DISCUSSION

1. Describe the organization of the receptive field mapped in this exercise. What is the term used to identify this arrangement? Why is that term appropriate?

2. Describe a neural circuit that would produce a ganglion cell's receptive field like that created by the automapping simulation.

Receptive Field Mapping

Single-cell recordings allowed researchers such as Hubel and Weisel to map the receptive fields of individual cells and to identify the response characteristics of those cells. Based on this type of research, several very different types of cells were identified, and important information about the architecture of the brain was developed.

Other than the requirement of a very, very small electrode capable of recording from single cells, the procedure used by Hubel and Weisel was a very low-tech one. They used a simple slide projector to present spots of light or line stimuli onto a screen in front of the research subject. They moved the projector as needed to vary stimulus location or orientation, and to introduce movement. The cell's activity was fed into an oscilloscope and amplifier so a visual signal and sound could be used to identify changes in the cell's response.

In this demonstration you will map several receptive fields. Read the introductory material and instructions provided in the demonstration before beginning. For each location (i.e., ganglion, LGN, cortex) select a stimulus (e.g., small spot, vertical line, etc.) and move the stimulus until you see or hear a change in the cell's response. Press the space bar to activate the "pencil," and click your mouse to mark the spot. Press the bar again to return to the stimulus. Continue this process until two receptive fields are mapped. Print out your results for each location in the visual pathway.

RESULTS & DISCUSSION

1. Provide your print-outs, and identify each type of receptive field. How accurate were your maps? Did the receptive fields correspond to what you expected at each level?

2. How did the type of stimulus influence your ability to get an accurate map of the receptive field? When was a movement required? When was direction important?

3. Did your maps reflect both excitatory and inhibitory areas?

Stimulus Size and Receptive Fields

For most receptive fields, stimulation in different regions of the receptive field may result in different responses by the cell. For example, cells with receptive fields with an on center-off surround organization produce an excitatory response when stimulated in the central region, but an inhibitory response when stimulated in the outer region. This exercise examines how stimulus size affects the response. Remember, the cell's response will reflect the total input it receives, so stimulus size may be important in determining the eventual response.

Be sure to note the firing rate when the cell is not being stimulated in addition to during stimulation. Pay attention to any changes in the firing rate as the size of the stimulus increases or decreases. Click on the different numbers to change the size of the stimulus. To view the same simulation with a receptive field of the opposite organization, click on the INHIBITORY CENTER button.

RESULTS & DISCUSSION

1. For the excitatory center receptive field, report the firing rate at baseline and for each stimulus size. Why did the rates change in this way?

2. When would a small stimulus produce the same response as a large stimulus?

3. If a cell is firing at its known baseline rate, do we know for sure that it is not being stimulated? Explain your answer.

Receptive Fields and Stimulus Size and Shape

The response of a ganglion cell depends on the total input it receives. Stimuli of different sizes, shapes, or general orientation may stimulate different amounts and different areas of the receptive field, so the input to the ganglion cell may vary widely. Because receptive fields also vary in size, stimuli of identical characteristics may sometimes produce very different responses in different ganglion cells.

This exercise allows you to observe how the size of a stimulus affects the neuron's response, and also how receptive field size influences the response. Unlike some of the previous exercises, the stimulus here is a bar, rather than a spot. This is especially appropriate because our environments produce many edge-like stimuli. You will have the opportunity to see the pattern of response that occurs with that shape stimulus.

Begin this exercise by manipulating the size of the stimulus, rather than the size of the receptive field. Note the baseline firing rate, and how the firing rate changes as the stimulus size is increased. After you understand this situation, reset the simulation and examine the pattern of response that occurs when a stimulus remains a constant size and the size of the receptive field changes.

RESULTS & DISCUSSION

1. How did the firing rate change as the width of the stimulus increased? How did the firing rate change when the stimulus remained the same, but receptive fields of different sizes were involved?

2. What general principle determines the response by the neuron? Why will stimulus shape be important, in addition to total size?

The Visual Pathways

There is a specific sequence of structures in the visual pathway through which visual information is transmitted. However, the exact path from eye to brain depends on where in the environment the stimulus originates. Becoming familiar with these structures, and understanding the specific paths stimuli follow will be very important for understanding some of the research to be discussed later.

In this exercise you will be asked to label the different structures in the visual pathway and to identify the right and left visual fields. Drag and drop the structure that corresponds to each location in the visual pathway. If you are wrong, your answer won't stick. To see how information from one visual field travels along the visual pathway to the brain, click on the dot under the left visual field. Pay special attention to the spatial relations of input from the left and right visual fields. Clicking on audio or script will present an explanation of this pathway.

RESULTS & DISCUSSION

1. Identify, in order, the major structures in the neural pathway for vision.

2. How does the original location of a stimulus in the environment relate to stimulus location in the eye and cortex?

3. At what structure does the neural pathway begin to include information from both the left and right eyes?

Simple Cells in the Cortex

The receptive fields of ganglion cells tend to have a center-surround organization, with a roughly round shape. For the excitatory-center type, maximum responses occur to a small spot of light that falls in the center of the receptive field. Other stimuli produce less than maximum responses or even an inhibitory response. Research by Hubel and Weisel established that the receptive fields for cortical cells, however, tend to have an elongated, side-by-side organization of the excitatory and inhibitory areas. As a result, stimuli such as lines are an ideal stimulus for these cells.

Simple cells differ in another regard, also. The side-by-side organization causes these cells to have a preferred orientation. The stimulus must be appropriately oriented (e.g., vertical, horizontal, etc.) to generate the maximum response. Stimuli in other orientations produce weaker responses.

This demonstration simulates the activity generated in a typical simple cortical cell when the orientation of a line stimulus is varied. Be sure to notice how firing rate changes as you change the line's orientation.

RESULTS & DISCUSSION

1. Describe the cell's response to the line when it was presented in a vertical, horizontal, and oblique (e.g., 45°) orientation.

2. What receptive field format would produce this orientation preference? What organization would be associated with the opposite orientation preference?

3. Simple cortical cells receive input from cells in the lateral geniculate nucleus (LGN). LGN cells have receptive fields that are similar in organization to those of the ganglion cells. How might LGN cells be organized in a neural circuit to produce the receptive field characteristic of a simple cortical cell?

Complex Cells in the Cortex

Simple cells respond selectively based on the orientation of line-like stimuli. Complex cells add another level of specificity and respond to a more narrowly defined range of stimuli. Complex cells have receptive fields that resemble those of simple cortical cells, but a stationary stimulus in a preferred orientation does not produce a strong response. Complex cells are selective not only for line orientation, but also for motion. There is another type of cortical cell, the end-stopped (or hypercomplex) cell, that is even more selective. End-stopped cells respond maximally when the stimulus is in a preferred orientation, is moving, and has a specific form – in many cases a specific length.

In this demonstration you will see the output of a complex cortical cell to stimuli of different orientations and different directions of movement. Click on the arrows at the bottom of the stimulus display to initiate movement. Be sure to see what happens for both directions.

RESULTS & DISCUSSION

1. Report the cell's response to lines of each orientation and movement combination. Which orientation produced the greatest response? Was motion important, and did the direction matter? How would this cell's preferred stimulus be described?

2. How might the neural circuit for this complex cortical cell be constructed using simple cortical cells?

3. Cells located farther along the visual pathway become more selective in terms of the stimulus characteristics that must be present in order for a response to occur. At the lowest levels, cells respond to simple spots of light. At the next level they respond to lines of a particular orientation. Farther yet, they respond to lines of a specific orientation and motion. Is it reasonable to think there may be brain cells that are so highly selective they represent crude "dog detectors" or "human face detectors," or be selectively responsive to some other very complex stimulus? Explain your answer.

Calculating Grating Contrast

The research by Hubel and Weisel on the organization of cortical cells provides support for the idea that cortical neurons may act as simple feature detectors in a pattern perception system. The basic features usually are considered lines of various orientations and simple combinations. However, another approach to pattern perception proposes that the basic component is the spatial frequency of intensity variations. According to this view, cortical neurons respond selectively to spatial frequency, not to line features.

Spatial frequency research often involves grating stimuli composed of bars of different intensities, contrasts (the difference in light intensity), and sizes (spatial frequency). Thus, high contrast gratings have alternating bars that are very different in intensity, and low contrast gratings have bars that are similar in intensity. One way to represent the contrast of a stimulus is Michaelson's contrast ratio.

In this exercise, you will manipulate the maximum and minimum intensity levels in a grating, and Michaelson's contrast ratio is computed for each condition. Always be sure to select a maximum intensity level that is at least as great as the minimum level you have selected. Note how the appearance of the grating changes as contrast changes and how the contrast ratio varies. Also pay attention to the plot of the grating as contrast is varied.

RESULTS & DISCUSSION

1. What is the formula for Michaelson's contrast ratio?

2. As the contrast ratio decreased, how did the appearance of the grating change?

3. Michaelson's contrast ratio for a grating with minimum and maximum values of 4 and 8 is the same as that of a grating with minimum and maximum values of 6 and 12. Does this mean the two grating look the same? Explain your answer.

Contrast Sensitivity

Contrast sensitivity is the ability to detect contrast, changes in brightness in a pattern. Contrast sensitivity is one measure of the quality of vision. Although it is very important for optimum visual behavior in the real world, it is not typically tested as part of a routine eye exam (perhaps because it cannot be corrected). It does, however, serve as a diagnostic sign for some health problems, and it is very useful in predicting visual performance in poor quality visual environments (such as landing an airplane in foggy conditions).

Contrast sensitivity is measured using any of the standard psychophysical techniques. Here, the method of adjustment and a forced-choice staircase version of the method of limits are used. In the method of adjustment, the observer adjusts a marker (or the stimulus itself in other versions) to the point that the sinewave grating is no longer visible (zero contrast). In the method of limits, the contrast is increased or decreased until the observer's response changes.

This experiment allows you to test your contrast sensitivity for four different spatial frequencies. Previous research clearly indicates that contrast sensitivity varies with spatial frequency. Very high spatial frequencies and very low spatial frequencies are usually associated with lower contrast sensitivity than mid-range values. Determine your contrast sensitivity as a function of spatial frequency using both the method of adjustment and the method of limits. Be sure to read the instructions and do some practice trials.

RESULTS & DISCUSSION

1. Present your data from each psychophysical method. Compare the two contrast sensitivity functions. Can you explain why any differences occurred?

2. Did your contrast sensitivity vary with spatial frequency? Which spatial frequencies have the highest contrast thresholds?

3. Some middle-aged people find they can read small print when they have good lighting, but that they need reading glasses if the light level is low. How might this be explained?

Orientation Aftereffect

Many aftereffects seem to be associated with systems that compare the output of cells that are selective to specific stimulus characteristics. You've learned that there are orientation-selective cells in the visual cortex, so you shouldn't be surprised that orientation aftereffects exist.

In this demonstration you will see two sinewave gratings that differ in orientation. You should note the orientation of each grating, and then look at the white bar that is located between the two gratings. After the adaptation period has ended, the tilted gratings will be replaced by two vertical gratings. Keep looking at the white bar, but note whether the vertical gratings both look vertical.

RESULTS & DISCUSSION

1. Did the vertical gratings look vertical, or did they appear tilted? How did any tilt relate to the tilt of the corresponding adaptation stimulus?

2. Try to explain this aftereffect.

Size Aftereffect

Although much of the research on pattern recognition refers to cortical cells that are responsive to lines of particular orientations, other research suggests that cortical cells are selective for spatial frequencies. Spatial frequency theory suggests that patterns are composed of complex waveforms of light and dark that can be broken down into their simple sinewave components. Some of the components are low spatial frequency (few cycles per unit of space, leading to gratings with wide bands) and some are high spatial frequency (many cycles per unit of space, leading to gratings with narrow bands).

In this demonstration you will see two sinewave gratings, one above and one below a small white bar. The two gratings will vary in spatial frequency. Look at the white bar during the adaptation period. When adaptation ends, the high and low frequency gratings will be replaced by two identical gratings of an intermediate spatial frequency. Keep looking at the white bar, but compare the two identical gratings, and be especially watchful for differences in size.

RESULTS & DISCUSSION

1. Describe the adaptation gratings. How did the two identical test gratings appear? Were they the same size (same spatial frequency)?

2. If there are cells tuned to respond to particular spatial frequencies, what does this aftereffect imply about those cells?

An alternative, or additional, approach to pattern perception is the spatial frequency analysis view. This approach proposes that a visual pattern may be considered a very complex combination of sinewave variations in lightness across space, and that the pattern recognition system extracts information about these waveforms – spatial frequency analysis. To begin to understand the spatial frequency approach to perception, you must understand how sine waves are combined and how these complex waveforms represent lightness.

This section of the *Spatial Vision* exercises permits you to explore how sine waves may be combined, what the resulting complex waveforms look like, and how this translates to variations in lightness. If you are unfamiliar with sine functions, begin by manipulating the amplitude of the initial function and observe how the waveform changes (click PLOT to plot the new waveform). Continue by adding one more frequency and observe how it changes the function. Continue adding frequencies and varying amplitudes until you understand how complex waves are formed. Be sure to pay attention to the grating shown in the box on the bottom so that you learn how spatial frequency represents lightness variations.

RESULTS & DISCUSSION

1. Explain what is meant by spatial frequency. To what does "spatial" refer?

2. How does a high amplitude, high frequency grating differ from a low amplitude, high frequency grating? How does a high amplitude, high frequency grating differ from a high amplitude, low frequency grating?

3. What is necessary to produce a square wave?

Spatial Vision, continued
Filter

Filters allow only certain components to pass through a system. In terms of spatial frequency analysis, the filter refers to blocking certain spatial frequencies. Filters may be described as low pass, meaning they allow only low frequencies through, or high pass, meaning they allow only high frequencies through. Although filters may be mechanical ones used to create stimuli, they also may represent the characteristics of biological systems involved in perception.

In this exercise, the characteristics of filters may be manipulated and the image that results observed. Select a beginning image and one of the types of filters. Move the cursor under the grating to select the range of frequencies the filter will pass. Click on FILTER IMAGE to activate the filter, then observe how the image changes. Try various frequency ranges and filter types until you understand how eliminating high, low, or mid-range spatial frequencies influences the appearance of an image. Change the filter efficiency to see how this variable influences the appearance of an image.

RESULTS & DISCUSSION

1. What happens to an image when high spatial frequencies are eliminated? Low spatial frequencies?

2. Cataracts make seeing fine details and sharp contours very difficult. What type of filter produces an image most similar to this? What type of filters produce visual effects similar to those seen in glaucoma, early Alzheimers, and multiple sclerosis?

Spatial Vision, continued
Subsample

Subsampling manipulates the "grain" of an image. Subsampling specifies the size of the area that is analyzed as one point. Within each area sampled, the levels of lightness are averaged, and that average then is used to represent that area. Thus, the amount of detail that is available for analysis will depend on the sampling function. In addition to averaging, subsampling tends to add high frequency components to the image. The high frequency components occur because of the edges of each sample block. This also may distort the image.

In this exercise you should select an original image from the list, manipulate the sampling size, and observe how the image changes. Click on SUBSAMPLE IMAGE to initiate the reformulation of the image. Note the specific characteristics of the image that are lost as sample size increases, and at what point the image becomes very difficult to recognize. Find a sampling level that greatly degrades the image but doesn't make it totally unrecognizable, and squint as you view the image. (Squinting reduces high frequencies.) Note how the image appears under those conditions. Repeat this exercise using one or two additional images so that you get a full appreciation for the concept.

RESULTS & DISCUSSION

1. Report your observations about the impact of sample size on the images you selected. At what sampling level did the images become very difficult to recognize?

2. How did squinting influence the appearance of the images? Why does this change occur?

Chapter 4: The Organized Brain

Virtual Labs for Chapter 4:

What and Where Streams
Tilt Illusion, 25 Degrees
Tilt Illusion, 75 Degrees
Bimodal Cell Responding

What and Where Streams

Visual input initially goes to the primary visual cortex (V1) where much of the most basic processing occurs. However, V1 is not the end of the line for visual input. More complex processing, such as that which results in object recognition, occurs in other cortical areas, the extrastriate cortex. Research using individuals with brain injuries in the extrastriate cortex has shown that two different pathways beyond V1 exist, and that the focus of processing differs in each pathway. These pathways are known as the ventral pathway and the dorsal pathway. The ventral pathway is primarily involved in pattern identification – determining *what* a stimulus represents. The dorsal pathway is involved in identifying the location of the stimulus or *how* to interact with the stimulus. Based on these different functions, the ventral pathway is sometimes called the "what" pathway, and the dorsal pathway is sometimes called the "where" or "how" or "action" pathway.

This exercise requires you to label the different pathways and the brain areas involved. Drag and drop each label to its appropriate location.

RESULTS & DISCUSSION

1. Where do both pathways originate? To which cortical area does the dorsal pathway go? The ventral pathway?

2. Why does it make sense that the dorsal pathway is the "action" pathway? (Hint: Consider the brain area that usually will be involved in "action."

3. If different aspects of processing occur in different pathways, and yet, we normally have a unified perception, what other kinds of pathways must exist?

Tilt Illusion, 25 Degrees

Tilt illusions occur when the angle of lines in a central figure are influenced by the angle of lines in the background. For some angles, the induced tilt is away from the angle of the background lines (direct tilt illusion), but for others the induced tilt is toward the angle of the background lines (indirect tilt illusion).

This demonstration presents a tilt illusion figure with a background of lines at 25° angles, and central figures composed of vertical lines. Judge the orientation of the lines in the center. Try rotating your head to the side and viewing the figures from a sideways perspective to explore whether the tilt illusion requires the test lines to be vertical.

RESULTS & DISCUSSION

1. Describe your perception of the lines when viewed normally.

2. Does the illusion also appear when the figure is viewed sideways and the test lines are horizontal instead of vertical?

Tilt Illusion, 75 Degrees

The perceived orientation of one region of line stimuli may be influenced by the orientation of lines appearing in the background. Lines may appear to be tilted away from, or toward, the angle of the background.

This demonstration presents a tilt illusion stimulus with background of lines at 75° angles, and central figures composed of vertical lines. Judge the orientation of the lines in the center.

RESULTS & DISCUSSION

1. Describe your perception of the lines.

2. Why do you think the background influences the perceived orientation of the central stimulus?

3. Compare the illusion in this exercise with that observed in the related exercise, *Tilt Illusion, 25 Degrees*. If the illusion is not the same with background lines of different orientations, why do you think this difference occurs?

Bimodal Cell Responding

When a neuron responds to stimulation within either of two senses, it is called a bimodal neuron (or multimodal, if more than two senses are involved). Graziano and Gross studied a certain subset of bimodal neurons classified as body-centered neurons located in the parietal lobe of monkeys. These neurons respond to either tactile (touch) stimuli or visual stimuli. However, not just any visual stimulus or tactile stimulus generates a response. The tactile response occurs only when a specific body part is stimulated, and the visual stimulus must be in an appropriate spatial relationship to that body part.

This demonstration illustrates how a bimodal neuron like those studied by Graziano and Gross operate. Follow the instructions provided, and be sure to listen (or read) the explanation provided. Make sure you understand what is meant by body-centered and why this neuron's behavior falls into that category.

RESULTS & DISCUSSION

1. When did tactile stimulation cause the neuron to fire? When did visual stimulation produce activity?

2. Explain why this neuron is "body-centered."

3. These neurons are found in the parietal lobe. Why is that location not surprising? Do you think this type of neuron is receiving input via the dorsal or the ventral visual pathways? Why?

Chapter 5: Perceiving Objects

Virtual Labs for Chapter 5:

Linear and Curved Illusory Contours
Enhancing Illusory Contours
Illusory Contours
Necker Cube
Schröder Stairs
Rabbit-Duck Demonstration
Young Girl-Old Woman
Hering Illusion
Converse Hering Illusion
Poggendorf Illusion
Law of Simplicity or Good Figure
Law of Similarity
Law of Good Continuation
Law of Proximity
Law of Common Fate
Law of Closure
Faces-Goblet
Real-World Figure-Ground Ambiguity
Figure-Ground Ambiguity
Shape from Shading – 3D Face
Global Precedence

Linear and Curved Illusory Contours

The Gestalt approach to perception often is described as asserting that "the whole is not equal to the sum of its parts." In other words, something more than the individual components of the sensory input determines perception. One phenomenon that illustrates this is the illusory, or subjective, contour. An illusory contour exists when the observer perceives an edge, or even an entire figure, that is not really present. Illusory contours tend to be perceived when the stimulus suggests some object is occluding parts of the display. The illusory contours define that object. This phenomenon is consistent with the Gestalt approach because it shows the arrangement of the entire stimulus display influences parts of that display. Although no single explanation has complete acceptance, cognitive influences appear to be influential.

This exercise provides examples of illusory contours and demonstrates how the characteristics of the display influence the contours. Examples of both straight and curved illusory contours are provided. Be sure to note how the contours change as objects are modified. Note that complex contours are possible.

RESULTS & DISCUSSION

1. For the straight contour display, describe the illusory contours in the basic figure, without apparent occlusion, and without the spheres. Did the brightness of the illusory figure differ from the rest of the field, and was it constant across the different conditions?

2. Describe what you saw in the curved contour figure. What was changed to produce curved contours?

3. Describe the complex illusory contour in the final figure.

4. Based on these demonstrations, what do you think causes illusory contours and their specific forms?

Enhancing Illusory Contours

The strength of illusory contours is dependent on the specific characteristics of the stimulus display. Adding appropriate information can significantly enhance the appearance of the illusory contours or change the perceived characteristics of the illusory surface.

In this demonstration, add each extra component separately, and note the impact on the illusory contours. Pay attention to the strength of the illusory contours and the appearance of the illusory surface. Try to determine the principles behind the enhancement effect.

RESULTS & DISCUSSION

1. Describe the impact of each addition to the display. Which ones resulted in the most enhancement?

2. What variation in the display caused the illusory surface to appear transparent, rather than solid?

3. What general principle do you think explains these enhancement effects?

Illusory Contours

Some figures are perceived because they are physically present in a stimulus. Others are perceived when the stimulus *suggests* their presence, even if they do not really exist. The latter situation describes the conditions in which illusory contours are observed. Illusory contours are borders that are perceived but are not real. Illusory contours often are perceived when the actual figure has "missing" parts that suggest it is being partially occluded. The occluding figure's contours are perceived as brighter regions than the rest of the field, even though the figure does not really exist.

Three different illusory contour figures are presented in this demonstration. Pay attention to the characteristics of the stimulus that induce the perception of the nonexistent figure. Think about what illusory contours suggest about pattern perception and the role of the physical stimulus. .

RESULTS & DISCUSSION

1. Describe the illusory contours you observed in the three figures.

2. How might Gestalt psychologists explain illusory contours?

3. What do illusory contours tell us about perception (other than it can be inaccurate)?

Necker Cube

The Necker cube represents a type of bistable figure in which perspective reverses. The identity of figure and ground is stable, but the position or orientation of the figure is subject to change. As with other bistable figures, a perceptual change occurs without any change in the stimulus itself.

In this exercise you will see two version of the Necker cube. For each, note which perspective you see first and the number of reversals you observe over approximately 30 seconds.

RESULTS & DISCUSSION

1. Report the perspective you first observed for each figure. How frequently did reversals occur for each? Was one perspective dominant?

2. Why do you think the Necker cube alternates in perspective?

3. What does the Necker Cube contribute to the study of perception? Why is it included in almost every perception textbook?

Schröder Stairs

The Schröder stairs drawing represents a bistable figure in which repeated alternations of perspective are perceived. The identity of figure and ground is stable, but the position or orientation of the figure is subject to change. As with other bistable figures, the change in perception occurs without any change in the stimulus itself.

In this exercise you will see the Schröder stairs figure. Note which perspective you see first and the number of reversals you observe over approximately 30 seconds.

RESULTS & DISCUSSION

1. Report the perspective you first observed. How frequently did reversals occur? Was one perspective dominant?

2. Do you think experience influenced your perception of this figure?

3. Why are examples of bistable perception uncommon in the natural world?

Rabbit-Duck Demonstration

The rabbit-duck figure represents a type of bistable figure. In a bistable figure, the perception of the figure changes. What might initially be perceived as a rabbit later is perceived as a duck, or vice versa. With continued observation, the process reverses again.

As you view this figure, pay attention to which version you perceive first (e.g., rabbit or duck) and how frequently your perception alternates. Note whether one version is more stable than the other. Also, try viewing the pictures sideways (rotate your head to the side) to see if the effect is the same from that position.

RESULTS & DISCUSSION

1. Report your first impression of the figure and the frequency with which it changed. Was one perception more stable than the other?

2. Some people initially have difficulty seeing one of the two identities. Did you experience that? Why do you think this occurs?

3. Most objects are still easily identified when they have been rotated to a sideways position. How did changing the orientation affect the figure? Why do you think this occurred?

Young Girl-Old Woman

The young girl-old woman figure represents another type of bistable figure. In a bistable figure, the identity of the figure changes. What might initially be perceived as a young woman later is perceived as an old woman. With continued observation, the process then reverses.

As you view this figure, pay attention to which version you perceive first (e.g., young woman or old woman) and how frequently your perception alternates. Note whether one version is more stable than the other. Also, try viewing the pictures sideways (rotate your head to the side) to see if the effect is the same from that position.

RESULTS & DISCUSSION

1. Report your first impression of the figure and the frequency with which it changed. Was one perception more stable than the other?

2. Some people initially have difficulty seeing one of the two identities. Did you experience that? Why do you think this occurs?

3. Most objects are still easily identified when they have been rotated to a sideways position. How did changing the orientation affect the figure? Why do you think this occurred?

Hering Illusion

The Hering illusion involves a distortion of lines when the lines appear in the context of a radiating pattern. The lines appear to be bent even though they are perfectly straight. Although this illusion involves shape, rather than size, a similar depth cue theory has been proposed.

This exercise presents the standard Hering illusion figure. Notice how the lines are distorted and consider how a depth-based theory might explain these illusions.

RESULTS & DISCUSSION

1. Describe how the lines appeared in the Hering figure.

2. Explain this illusion using the theory that misleading depth cues are involved.

Converse Hering Illusion

The Converse Hering illusion is an alternate version of the standard Hering illusion. Again, there is a distortion of lines when lines appear in the context of a radiating pattern. The lines appear to be bent even though they are perfectly straight. Although this illusion involves shape, rather than size, a similar depth cue theory has been proposed.

This exercise presents the Converse Hering illusion figure developed by Wilhelm Wundt. Notice how the lines are distorted and consider how a depth-based theory might explain this illusion. Before beginning, click **?** (Help) to view some additional information.

RESULTS & DISCUSSION

1. Describe how the lines appeared in the Converse Hering illusion figure. Compare this version of the Hering illusion to that illustrated in the lab titled *Hering Illusion*.

2. Explain this illusion using the theory that misleading depth cues are involved.

Poggendorf Illusion

In the Poggendorf illusion, line segments intersect two vertical lines (or other figure) at an angle. When the two line segments are aligned so that they could represent one continuous straight line, they do not appear to be aligned. One line appears higher than the other.

As with other illusions, several theories have been proposed. One commonly cited theory suggests that the angles are misperceived because acute angles tend to be overestimated and obtuse angles tend to be underestimated. Another theory states that the figure is perceived as a 3-dimensional figure in which the two lines are on two different receding planes that form a right angle with the rectangle. Distorted perspective due in part to angle over- and under-estimation leads to the illusion. However, neither of these theories can account for all of the variants of the illusion.

This demonstration presents the standard Poggendorf illusion figure. Judge whether the two line segments are aligned to represent one continuous line. To check the alignment without the influence of the vertical lines, click on HIDE BACKGROUND.

RESULTS & DISCUSSION

1. Did the two lines look properly aligned? If not, how would you have adjusted the line on the right side?

2. Some researchers have noted that this illusion resembles a partial Muller-Lyer figure (note the angles created by the intersections of the lines). Use this idea to explain the Poggendorf illusion.

Law of Simplicity or Good Figure

A central idea in the Gestalt approach to perceptual organization is that we tend to organize our perceptual world so that figures are simple or "good." We tend to see the simplest arrangement of a display. This principle, also known as the Law of Pragnanz, is not independent of the other Gestalt laws, however. The other laws often lead to an organization in which the figures are simple and good, versus complex or irregular. For example, by ignoring gaps between curved segments (law of closure) to create a perception of a circle, rather than several irregularly sized curved lines, a good figure is perceived.

You surely are aware that the world is not always an orderly, simple place, and that objects can be quite complex or irregular. Thus, you probably will not be surprised to learn that at times the Gestalt law of simplicity or good figure will lead to an incorrect perception. In spite of the failures, however, the law of simplicity or good figure more often leads to the correct perception than to an incorrect one.

This lab illustrates one case in which the world does not conform to the Gestalt principle of good figure. See how your view of the stimulus display corresponds to the actual situation.

RESULTS & DISCUSSION

1. What did you perceive in the original display? What was revealed when the components of the display were separated?

2. We certainly can construct stimulus displays in which the Gestalt laws will result in incorrect perceptions. If these laws are fallible, why is our perception in the real world as accurate as it tends to be? When are we most likely to be led astray by the Gestalt laws? Give an example, if possible.

Law of Similarity

The Gestalt psychologists are known for their laws of perceptual organization. These laws identify several very basic principles that guide how the stimulus array is grouped or organized. Perhaps the most basic grouping that occurs is figure-ground relationship. That is, which parts of the stimulus array represent the background, and which parts represent objects (figures)? Within the stimuli that represent objects, where does one object end and another begin?

One of the laws of perceptual organization is the law of similarity. As its name implies, this law states that similar patterns tend to be grouped together or perceived to be part of the same, larger object. The characteristics that cause the strongest, most immediate grouping tend to be those that are basic sensory attributes that do not require a lot of interpretation, such a size, color, brightness, line orientation, etc.

In this exercise you will see how the organization of a stimulus array is affected by the similarity of the array's individual components. Note the organization of the array prior to adding a similarity component, and then see how the organization changes as you introduce two colors or other characteristics.

RESULTS & DISCUSSION

1. Describe your perception of the array prior to adding color. How did your perception change when some spheres were red and others were blue? What other variable was effective in changing the perceived organization?

2. What do you think would happen if the balls were randomly colored red or blue, rather than using rows or columns to assign color? Would grouping still occur?

3. Describe a real-world situation in which the law of similarity contributed to your perception.

Law of Good Continuation

The law of good continuation is one of the Gestalt principles of perceptual organization. This law states that a figure is organized so that its lines are straight or smoothly curved and follow the smoothest path. If the stimulus is composed of points, rather than lines, the points are organized so that if connected, the lines created will be straight or smoothly curved and follow the smoothest path.

This demonstration illustrates the impact of the law of good continuation. Before doing anything to change the display, note how you organize the complex pattern into parts. Then shift the cursor to separate the pattern into two components. Click on GOOD CONTINUATION and separate the parts again. Note your reaction to this organization.

RESULTS & DISCUSSION

1. How did you perceptually organize the original figure? Did the first separation confirm your expectations?

2. Describe how the pattern was organized in the GOOD CONTINUATION condition. How is this organization consistent with the law of good continuation?

3. Describe a real-world situation that is influenced by the law of good continuation.

Law of Proximity

The law of proximity states that stimuli that are close to one another tend to be grouped together. This makes sense because objects in the real world involve a prescribed region, not widely scattered points. Obviously, the law of proximity alone will not always be able to correctly organize figures in the perceptual array, because objects that are located close together would tend to be seen as one larger object. However, this law describes a general tendency that is most influential when other factors are equal. In many cases, several Gestalt principles and other sensory cues will interact to produce the final perceptual organization.

This exercise illustrates how the law of proximity works. Note how you would describe the stimulus array prior to making any adjustments. Next, vary the distance between the spheres and note how the organization of the array changes.

RESULTS & DISCUSSION

1. Report how the initial arrangement appeared. What happened when you varied the separation between the spheres?

2. Describe a situation in the real world in which the law of proximity is influential.

3. Why do we usually not confuse where one object begins and another ends, even if the objects are touching one another?

Law of Common Fate

The law of common fate introduces movement as a cue for perceptual organization. According to this Gestalt law, stimuli that move together tend to be grouped together. Stimuli that do not move in the same direction, or at the same speed, as others tend to be grouped separately.

This exercise illustrates how perceptual grouping is influenced by common fate. Note how the objects are organized when in motion. Click on CHANGE GROUPING to see different arrangements. Note whether the law of common fate overrides other Gestalt principles.

RESULTS & DISCUSSION

1. Why does the information provided with the demonstration suggest that the law of common fate overrides the law of proximity in this demonstration? Describe the situation that illustrates this idea.

2. Describe a real-world situation in which the law of common fate is in action.

Law of Closure

The law of closure states that figures tend to be perceived as complete, unbroken patterns. Small gaps or other missing parts often are ignored, and the figure is organized as it would be without those gaps. This is a very similar concept to the law of good continuation.

This exercise illustrates the law of closure. By clicking on the figures, small gaps will be introduced. Note whether your perception of the figure really changes. Obviously, you will be aware of the gaps, but does your perceptual organization of the figure change?

RESULTS & DISCUSSION

1. Describe your perception of the figures before and after the gaps were introduced. Did anything change? What do you think would happen if the gaps were more numerous or larger?

2. Describe a real-world situation in which the law of closure was at work.

Faces-Goblet

The faces-goblet figure may be the most famous figure-ground bistable pattern. The inner and outer portions of the pattern alternate between being perceived as figure and as ground. At one moment the inner region will appear to be a goblet figure, and the next, that same area will appear to be the background behind two faces in profile. Nothing has changed in the stimulus, but perception changes, regardless.

As you view this stimulus, note which part you first see as figure, and keep track of how frequently your perception changes over about 30 seconds of viewing time.

RESULTS & DISCUSSION

1. What did you first perceive as figure? Do you think your perception would be the same if the colors used in the pattern were reversed? Why or why not?

2. Report the frequency of figure-ground reversals you experienced. Was one organization more stable than the other? Why do you think these reversals occur?

Rubin's reversible face-vase figure is a classic example of ambiguous figure-ground perception. The normal cues used to segregate figure from ground are either not available or are in conflict. For example, a small area surrounded by a larger, uniform area tends to be seen as figure, and light areas tend to be judged as figures, suggesting the figure is the white vase. However, the black area contains meaningful forms related to faces in profile, suggesting the faces are the figures. As a result, figure and ground in this figure tend to reverse from one to another.

Figure-ground ambiguity is most common in artificial, scantily-detailed patterns. In most real-world situations there is enough information to prevent figure-ground ambiguity and reversals, but occasionally there are situations in which cues are in conflict and reversals occur. Such is the case of the Kaiser Porcelain Limited vase created for a wedding present for Queen Elizabeth II and the Duke of Edinburgh. Even though the object is the vase, the reversed perspective does occur under proper conditions.

This exercise demonstrates how figure-ground segregation can shift as information changes. Note your dominant perception when the initial high-contrast version is viewed. Move the cursor to change the contrast and details available in the different regions of the scene. Note how your perception changes and what seems to determine that change. Note whether you observe any figure-ground reversals when the vase is shown in detail.

RESULTS & DISCUSSION

1. What was the dominant figure-ground orientation of the initial version of the figure? Describe how this changed as the characteristics of the scene changed.

2. What features did you find most important in allowing the vase to be perceived as an object with little ambiguity. Why were reversals still possible?

3. Do you think you would have noticed the alternative figure-ground orientation for the version showing the picture of the wedding present if you were not primed to look for it?

Figure-Ground Ambiguity

Perception of a scene first requires a determination of what parts of the stimulus array represent background, or ground, and what parts represent objects, or figures. Object recognition may proceed only after this figure-ground separation is complete. How does the perceptual system differentiate between figure and ground? The Gestalt laws of perceptual organization may be influential in grouping together components in the stimulus array as a first step toward figure-ground segregation.

In some cases, the cues for figure-ground are limited or ambiguous. Escher, an artist, is well known for his pictures with ambiguous figure-ground relationships. A first look yields one view, but after a few moments the perception changes and the figure-ground relationship may reverse or otherwise dramatically change.

This lab provides an illustration of ambiguous figure-ground relationships using artwork by Bev Doolittle, and it allows you to see how contrast can influence figure-ground perception. Slide the cursor to adjust the scene's contrast, and note how low contrast changes figure-ground perception. Evaluate the cues you use to identify figure and ground in this picture. To get a better feel for how differences in contrast influence figure-ground segregation, manipulate the contrast of only the background.

RESULTS & DISCUSSION

1. How did contrast influence figure-ground perception? What happened when the contrast of only the ground was adjusted?

2. What cues allowed you to identify the figures in this ambiguous stimulus? Explain.

3. What real-world situation corresponds to the very low contrast conditions possible in this demonstration? How might these conditions influence behavior in addition to perception?

Shape from Shading – 3D Face

Shading is an important cue for depth and shape. For three-dimensional stimuli, shadows occur when surfaces do not directly face the light source or when other parts of the object block the light source. The position and depth of shading directly relate to the position of the light source and the shape of the object, so shading can help reveal shape.

This demonstration illustrates how shading influences shape perception. In addition, it illustrates how the assumptions about the lighting source, if incorrect, may lead to faulty perceptions.

RESULTS & DISCUSSION

1. Describe how the figure first appeared.

2. When the orientation of the figure changed, what was revealed?

3. Explain how information about lighting and shadows produced two different perceptions of the figure.

Global Precedence

Global precedence refers to the issue of whether information about the more global aspects of a stimulus is processed faster than information about the local characteristics (details) of the stimulus. Some researchers suggest that a global precedence effect might occur because global information is carried in the faster magnocellular pathway, and local information is carried by the slower parvocellular pathway.

Global and local processing frequently have been studied using stimuli composed of letters. Small letters are arranged to form a larger letter. All of the small letters are the same in a single stimulus, but the large letter varies. Research participants are asked to respond as to which letter is presented. In some conditions that response is made in reference to the large letters (global condition), and in other conditions the response is to the small letters (local condition). The letters that are irrelevant are often varied so that in some cases global and local information is consistent (both S) and in some cases inconsistent (small S arranged in an H). This variable allows the idea of faster global processing to be further tested.

In this experiment you will replicate an experiment originally conducted by Navon. The experiment uses reaction times to examine the difference in global and local processing. You should carefully read the instructions before beginning. Also, remember to respond as rapidly as possible, without making too many mistakes. Complete the practice trials so that you are familiar with the stimuli and procedures.

RESULTS & DISCUSSION

1. Report your data for both global and local processing conditions. How does global processing compare to local processing overall?

2. Does consistency make a difference? Is the consistency effect the same for both local and global processing? What does this suggest concerning the nature of the global precedence effect?

3. Reaction time data is very useful, but it must be interpreted carefully. If you were slower responding to one letter, what conclusions are possible? If you were faster in one condition than another, but you also made more errors in that condition, what problem does this create in interpreting your data?

Chapter 6: Visual Attention

Virtual Labs for Chapter 6:

Inattentional Blindness Stimuli
Change Blindness
Feature Analysis

Inattentional Blindness Stimuli

A tremendous amount of information enters the sensory system, but is all of it perceived? Is every object noticed and identified? Is every shadow and nuance of color recognized and used? The research of Mack and Rock suggests that the answer to these questions is, "No." They performed an experiment in which a cross was briefly presented and the observer's task was to report which of the arms appeared longer. In other words, the attention of the participants was directed to the cross, and everything else in the display was irrelevant to the task. Mack and Rock questioned whether the parts of the display not given any attention would be perceived. Although the entire display was clearly above threshold, and the observers were aware that the cross was not the only pattern on the screen, the observers could not provide much information about the stimuli not given specific attention. This lack of perception of unattended stimuli is known as inattentional blindness.

This exercise replicates the Mack and Rock procedure. Watch the display, and report which arm of the cross is longer. Without taking your eyes off the screen, make a mark on a sheet of paper to indicate your response. Focus your attention on the cross, not on any other aspect of the display. Don't read the questions in the RESULTS & DISCUSSION section below until after you have completed the exercise.

RESULTS & DISCUSSION

1. Report your answers concerning the longer arms of the crosses.

2. What, if anything, did you see in the display other than the cross stimulus? Did you see any forms? If so, what were they?

3. What does inattentional blindness tell us about visual perception?

Change Blindness

Change blindness is a phenomenon in which the observer does not perceive changes that occur very gradually. The total change can be quite substantial, and quite obvious, if completed quickly, but it will not be noticed when it occurs gradually.

This exercise presents three examples of change blindness. Select one of the pictures and click the forward arrow on the bar just under the picture to initiate the sequence. Watch very carefully and try to detect the change. To see the change in reverse and at higher speed, click the back arrow on the bar under the picture. After you know what changes, watch the sequence again and see if change blindness still occurs. Observe all three pictures. To read a brief explanation of this effect, click the green button on the right beneath the display.

RESULTS & DISCUSSION

1. For each picture, describe the change that occurred and what you observed.

2. Did knowing what to watch affect your ability to see the change as it developed?

3. Why do you think it is so hard to see graduate change? What does this phenomenon tell us about perception?

Feature Analysis

Most pattern recognition theories suggest that some sort of feature analysis is conducted. In other words, the basic components of a pattern are processed, and based on that information the pattern is identified. How quickly processing is completed depends on the nature of the pattern and its relationship to other patterns. Treisman noted that in some pattern processing tasks, a decision may be made quickly if the target has some unique feature that can be processed without focused attention. However, if the target shares features with non-target stimuli and may be recognized only after all aspects of the stimulus are processed, processing will require focused attention and will be slow.

This experiment uses a visual search task to explore the kinds of stimuli that may be processed preattentively versus those that require focused attention. In visual search tasks a target is defined, and the observer makes a "present"-"absent" response. Distractor stimuli also are presented, and the number of distractors may be varied. By comparing search times for trials with few distractors and for those with many distractors, conclusions about the nature of processing are possible. Other comparisons are useful for determining still more details about the pattern recognition process.

Before beginning this experiment, read the supporting information and instructions carefully and complete some practice trials. Repeat the experiment several times, selecting stimuli that are appropriate for testing issues of interest. Be sure to use patterns you suspect may be processed preattentively and others that you suspect require focused attention. Also, perform the task with one stimulus acting as target in one case and as distractor in another. Compare searching for the presence versus the absence of a primitive feature. The background information should give you additional ideas.

RESULTS & DISCUSSION

1. Report your results for each of the conditions you tested. What conclusions are possible?

2. Did the number of distractors affect search speed equally in all conditions? What do you conclude?

3. Were search times for "present" and "absent" trials similar in all conditions? What do you conclude?

Chapter 7: Perceiving Color

Virtual Labs for Chapter 7:

Color Mixing
Cone Response Profiles and Hue
Cone Response Profiles and Perceived Color
Color Arrangement Test
Rod Monochromacy
Dichromacy
Dichromats and Monochromats
Neutral Points in Dichromats
"Oh Say Can You See" Afterimage Demonstration
Color Contingent Motion
Motion Contingent Color
McCollough Effect
Simultaneous Color Contrast
Color Assimilation
Measuring Illusions
Simultaneous Contrast: Dynamic
Simultaneous Contrast: Static
Red-Green Opponent Cells
Missing Blue-Yellow Channel
Mixing Complimentary Colors
Strength of Blue-Yellow Mechanisms
Strength of Red-Green Mechanism
Opponent-Process Coding of Hue
Troxler Effect

Color Mixing

There are two types of color mixing: additive color mixing and subtractive color mixing. Subtractive color mixing involves removing wavelengths of light. This is what occurs when paints are mixed or colored filters are put over lights. The pigments allow only certain wavelengths to be reflected and reach the eye. Filters allow only certain wavelengths to pass through and proceed to the eye. The wavelengths that reach the eye determine the color perceived. In additive mixture, however, wavelengths are added to a mixture. This occurs when lights are combined or projected onto the same location. For additive mixture, three primary wavelengths of light may be mixed in appropriate proportions in order to create any hue desired.

In this demonstration, you have the opportunity to work with additive color mixture. Slide the cursor to adjust the amount of each primary color. The resulting mixture will be shown in the circle below the primaries, and its point in the color space will be mapped. Experiment with different combinations of the primaries. Try to create some target color (e.g., yellow), noting the specific values of each primary used. Change the level of one primary and see if you can get the same color by adjusting the other two primaries. Also, mix equal amounts of each primary and note the color produced and the location in its RGB color space. Repeat using different equal amounts (e.g., 200, 175, 150). Also try mixing colors using a different set of primaries (click on CMY). Be aware that different color spaces exist (RGB, CMY, HSB), and compare how mixtures are plotted in the different spaces. Look at the EXAMPLES page for more complete information.

RESULTS & DISCUSSION

1. What happened when you added equal amounts of the three primaries? As the amount of each primary was decreased, how did the appearance change, and how did the mixture's location change in the RGB and HSB color spaces?

2. Could you create the same color using different values of the three primaries? Explain.

3. Compare how hue and brightness are represented in the different color spaces.

Cone Response Profiles and Hue

The trichromatic theory of color vision states that the three types of cones are maximally sensitive to specific wavelengths of light, and that the output from each type of cone is used to determine a light's hue, much like the mathematical formula used in additive color mixture. Interestingly, the original trichromatic theory was based primarily on color mixing data because the physiology of the cones had not yet been established. More recent research confirmed the existence of the three types of cones.

This exercise produces response profiles for the three types of cones as a function of the wavelength of light. Drag the cursor across the spectrum, and note the level of response by each type of cone. The functions in the right figure represent the same information that is shown in the left panel. The left panel, however, shows a simple profile of response across the three types of cones for a particular wavelength of light.

RESULTS & DISCUSSION

1. Report the output for each of the three types of cones for the wavelengths 435 nm, 520 nm, and 560 nm, the wavelengths approximately corresponding to the peaks of the three cone functions.

2. Explain why the three types of cones are described as "short," "middle," and "long" wavelength cones, rather than in terms of "blue," "green," and "red."

Cone Response Profiles and Perceived Color

This lab has basically the same information as the previous lab. Rather than showing the entire spectrum, however, only selected colors are included. Response profiles for the three types of cones are again provided for each color selected.

The colors in this exercise are arranged in a color circle. The color circle was developed to represent not only the order of colors in the spectrum, but also how they relate for simple additive color mixing. The locations of two colors on the color circle can be used to predict the color of their mixture. The color circle in this exercise does not include the entire range of colors, so it cannot be used for that purpose, however. Also, even a complete color circle is inaccurate. The best representation of the color space is actually a rounded triangle-like shape.

Pay particular attention to the difference in the profiles for different colors. You might notice that some of the profiles in this exercise do not correspond exactly to those in your text. Use the ones in the text if the details of the profiles are required.

RESULTS & DISCUSSION

1. Report the response profiles for the wavelength that corresponds to a good example of blue, green, yellow, and red. Do they differ greatly?

2. The most extreme blue and the most extreme red produce activity in only one receptor. Green, however, produces a response in at least two receptors. Why?

Color Arrangement Test

Color deficiencies occur when at least one cone photopigment is either abnormal or missing. The common use of the term "color blind" refers to color vision in which one photopigment is missing, dichromacy, and this condition produces confusions between certain ranges of colors. When two photopigments are missing, monochromacy, the individual confuses all colors, and perception is achromatic (black, grey, white).

The Color Arrangement Test is one test of color vision. In this test, patches of colors must be arranged in their proper order. People with normal color vision have little difficulty with this test, and they rarely make many errors. People with color deficiencies, however, make significant errors, and the nature of their errors is diagnostic of the type of deficiency involved.

Take the Color Arrangement Test and check your results. Your results will be available in two forms: a graphic representation and a quantitative one that is more detailed in its diagnostic value. Print out your plotted results and the results table. Compare your results to those characteristic of the different color deficiencies. Be aware that your results might not be valid. The variation between the colors produced on different computers can be significant and this could distort the results of the test.

RESULTS & DISCUSSION

1. Provide a print-out of your results in both graphic and quantitative formats. Do your graphic results compare most closely to normal color vision? If not, which color deficiency produces results similar to yours?

2. What kinds of errors does a protanope make? A deuteranope? A tritanope?

Rod Monochromacy

There are three basic types of color deficiency: monochromacy, dichromacy, and anomalous trichromacy. The first two types of color deficiency are caused by the absence of one or more photopigment. Anomalous trichromacy involves an abnormal photopigment, rather than a missing one. Of the three types of color deficiency, monochromacy is the most severe and the least common. In rod monochromacy, the retina contains only rods, and thus, there is only one type of photopigment. With only one type of photopigment, perception is limited to variations in intensity. The rod photopigment does react differently as a function of the wavelength of the light, but without a second photopigment with a different spectral sensitivity function, differences in wavelength cannot be differentiated from differences in intensity. The result is a lack of color perception.

This exercise allows you to see how the visual spectrum appears to a rod monochromat and provides information about the frequency of the condition in the general population. Also be sure to note the differences in the visual perception of a rod monochromat other than color deficiency.

RESULTS & DISCUSSION

1. Describe how the visible spectrum appears to a rod monochromat. Why do some wavelengths produce different responses than others?

2. How frequent is rod monochromacy in the general population? Is there any difference in the frequency within the male and female populations?

3. How does the rod monochromat's vision differ from that of a person with the normal complement of visual receptors? Why does this difference occur?

Dichromacy

The term "color blind" more appropriately describes the vision of rod monochromats, but it almost always is used to refer to the color deficiency of dichromacy. Dichromats, unlike monochromats, do see color, but their color perception is very different from that of people with normal trichromacy. In dichromacy, the retina contains both rods and cones. Rather than three distinctly different types of cone photopigments, though, there are only two. This allows some color vision, but the range of colors perceived and the relationship of perceived color to wavelength are quite abnormal. The specific type of cone that is absent in the dichromat will vary from person to person, but the most common forms of dichromacy are protanopia and deuteranopia. Protanopia is characterized by the lack of cones containing the long-wavelength pigment, deuteranopia is characterized by the lack of cones containing the middle-wavelength pigment, and tritanopia, although not well understood, is probably characterized by the lack of the cones containing the short-wavelength pigment. The specific colors that are lost and the relationship of wavelength to the colors perceived depends on which type of photopigment is missing.

This exercise illustrates color perception in dichromacy. Click on one cone at a time to see the result of removing that type of cone. Pay attention to the colors perceived, how they correspond to wavelength, and the frequency of the disorder in the population. Also, be sure to note the wavelength shown somewhere in the middle of the spectrum that represents the neutral point.

RESULTS & DISCUSSION

1. For each type of cone photopigment, describe the color perception that is possible when that photopigment is missing and how the perceived colors relate to wavelength.

2. What are the neutral points for protanopia, deuteranopia, and tritanopia, and what is perceived at these neutral points?

3. How common are these forms of color deficiency? Are males and females equally likely to be dichromats? Why or why not?

Dichromats and Monochromats

Although their color vision is very abnormal, dichromats do perceive color, unlike monochromats. This demonstration compares how a scene is perceived by monochromats and the three types of dichromats. Carefully examine all the regions of the scene, and notice which colors are perceived most abnormally.

RESULTS & DISCUSSION

1. Compare the way the scene appears to people with each of the types of color deficiency. (Describe which colors are confused.)

2. Why are some areas seen as black or almost black?

3. Which condition do you think would create the most difficulty in daily life? Explain your decision.

Neutral Points in Dichromats

Dichromats, people who lack one of the three types of cone photopigments, do see colors, but only a restricted range of colors. There is a point in the spectrum, however, that appears achromatic to them. This neutral point is different for each of the three versions of dichromacy.

This exercise identifies the neutral point for each type of dichromacy. Click on the protanope's and deuteranope's color spectrum, and note the location of the neutral point for each. Proceed to the next page to see where this point is located relative to the region of inactivity in the blue-yellow opponent system. Continue to the simulation of tritanopia and repeat the process, this time comparing the neutral point to the red-green opponent system's response function.

RESULTS & DISCUSSION

1. What are the neutral points for each of the types of dichromacy? How do they compare to points of no activity for the intact opponent system?

2. Why is vision achromatic at these neutral points?

3. Why is there only one neutral point for tritanopes?

4. Do you think real-world vision is affected by the presence of these neutral points? Why or why not?

Afterimages are illusory perceptions that are caused by fatigued receptors. Intense or prolonged stimulation of a specific area of the retina temporarily fatigues receptors in that area and reduces their output. For example, when a flash unit is used to take a photograph, you often will see a dark spot in your vision for a short period of time. That dark spot is an afterimage of the flash. The receptors most affected by the flash are fatigued, and their response to subsequent stimulation will be reduced relative to that of receptors in other areas. This low activity level is interpreted to reflect an area of low stimulation, and thus, a dark spot.

Afterimages also may be colored, and their colors will be "opposite" that of the original stimulus (e.g., red – green). In the 1800's Hering noted that the pairing of colors in several color phenomena, including afterimages, was quite consistent, with red paired with green and blue paired with yellow, most notably. These observations, and the realization that trichromatic theory cannot explain these phenomena and these pairings, contributed to the formulation of Hering's opponent process theory of color perception.

This lab will allow you to experience a colored negative afterimage. Stare at the center of the figure for one minute, noting the colors, then click on the background (not the button!). You should see an afterimage of the figure. Note the colors in the afterimage. Click on the button to see a comparison of the original and afterimage.

RESULTS & DISCUSSION

1. Describe the original stimulus, including its colors. Describe the afterimage, including its colors. Did the afterimage's color match the predictions Hering's opponent process theory would make?

2. Explain how the opponent process theory explains negative afterimages like this one.

3. Why does this phenomenon create problems for the trichromatic theory of color vision?

Color Contingent Motion

In some of the other demonstrations you have adapted with one eye and looked for aftereffects with the other. When the aftereffect is seen with an unadapted eye, the effect originates in the brain instead of in the eye. Also, the explanation given for most aftereffects refers to systems that rely on a comparison of the output of two channels of input that are each maximally responsive to specific stimulus characteristics.

In this lab two red/green gratings moving in opposite directions are presented above and below a small white fixation bar. After the adaptation period ends, one grating will be replaced by a blue/yellow grating and both gratings will stop moving. Continue looking at the white bar, but watch for any movement aftereffect. Pay particular attention to the strength and duration of the aftereffects. Note whether the motion aftereffect seen for the red/green grating is the same strength and duration as that seen for the blue/yellow grating.

RESULTS & DISCUSSION

1. Describe any aftereffect you observed in the test gratings, and compare this to the adaptation gratings.

2. Was the aftereffect equally strong and long-lasting with the red/green and blue/yellow gratings?

3. Is this effect surprising? Provide a possible explanation, and discuss what this aftereffect suggests about the color and motion systems.

Motion Contingent Color

The previous lab showed that motion aftereffects may be contingent upon the test stimulus being a particular color. This demonstration shows that color aftereffects may be contingent on a test stimulus that moves in a particular direction.

In this lab, two sine wave gratings are alternated during an adaptation period. One grating is red and the other is green. Note the direction each grating is moving. Look at the small white fixation bar that appears in the middle of the display. The adaptation period is quite long, but this is necessary for the aftereffect to be visible. When the adaptation period is complete, the colored gratings will be replaced by two identical grey gratings moving in opposite directions, one above the white bar and one below it. Keep looking at the white fixation bar during the test period. Look for any color that is visible in the two gratings.

RESULTS & DISCUSSION

1. Describe the aftereffect you experienced for the right-moving (top) and the left-moving (bottom) test stimulus gratings. How did the color relate to that of the adaptation stimulus?

2. This aftereffect reportedly is very long-lasting when adaptation is sufficient. Is this a potential problem for standard explanations of aftereffects? Why or why not?

McCollough Effect

The McCollough effect is an orientation-contingent color aftereffect. The color aftereffect is tightly linked to the orientation of the adaptation and test stimuli. Like the motion contingent aftereffect, the McCollough effect requires a considerably longer adaptation period than many other aftereffects, and it can be very long lasting. As a result, explanations for the McCollough effect have had to expand beyond the more traditional theories of color aftereffects. Some theories even include a Pavlovian conditioning factor.

In this demonstration of the McCollough effect, a vertical, red grating and a horizontal, green grating are alternated. The adaptation period is long, but don't be tempted to terminate it early. The lengthy adaptation is necessary. For testing the aftereffect, a black and white stimulus composed of both vertical and horizontal bars is presented. Notice any color that appears and the orientation of the bars in that region. Also note how long the aftereffect remains visible.

RESULTS & DISCUSSION

1. Describe the aftereffect you experienced. Was the color of the aftereffect linked to a specific orientation? How did this compare to the color of the adaptation stimulus of that orientation?

2. How long did the aftereffect remain visible?

3. This aftereffect required a much longer adaptation period than many other aftereffects. What does that suggest about the origin of the aftereffect?

Simultaneous Color Contrast

Simultaneous contrast is not limited to the dimension of lightness or brightness. The context in which a stimulus occurs also influences the color it appears, color contrast. Color contrast effects typically are produced when a neutral (grey) figure is presented on a colored background. The neutral figure takes on a color because of the color of the background.

In this demonstration a small, mostly neutral (actually slightly yellow-grey) circle moves across a background that varies from blue to yellow. Pay attention to the color of the circle and any other changes that occur. To prove to yourself that the circle does not change, change the background to one solid color.

RESULTS & DISCUSSION

1. What color was the dot when in the blue region? When in the yellow? Why do these colors occur? If the background had been green, what color would the circle have been?

2. What do you think causes color contrast?

3. Describe the other change in the circle's appearance. What does this change represent?

Color Assimilation

Assimilation effects occur when the characteristics of one area are incorporated into nearby areas. Thus, assimilation is the opposite of contrast. One common form of assimilation involves the spreading of color to other regions. That is, a red region may cause nearby areas also to appear red. Some research indicates that assimilation is more likely to occur for a stimulus that is perceived to be the background than for stimuli perceived to be figures. In comparison, contrast tends to occur when the stimulus is perceived to be the figure, rather than the background.

In this demonstration you will see four narrow grey bars moving up and down a field that changes from red to green. Notice the color of the bars as they move from one region to another.

RESULTS & DISCUSSION

1. Report what you observed in this demonstration. Did assimilation occur?

2. Does this demonstration support the idea that assimilation occurs for background, and contrast for figures?

3. Are there benefits to assimilation?

Measuring Illusions

Perceptual illusions are interesting in their own right, but they also may provide good information about how the perceptual system works. As a result, researchers have tried to understand the origins of many perceptual illusions and the variables that affect them. In this experiment you have the opportunity to measure the strength of three illusions under different conditions and to see how the method of limits is used in real research. The three illusions are the Muller-Lyer illusion, the vertical-horizontal illusion, and simultaneous brightness contrast.

In each version of this experiment you will be asked to make a YES-NO judgment comparing two stimuli. Be sure to pay attention to the question being asked, and don't miss the briefly presented stimulus. Also, wait until the YES and NO buttons are no longer dimmed, or your response will not register. Print out your data for each condition and each illusion, and save it to a file until you have completed this exercise.

Muller-Lyer Illusion

One factor thought to influence the Muller-Lyer illusion is misleading depth information. By manipulating the length of the arrowheads on the ends of the lines, the impact of the linear perspective depth cue may be emphasized or diminished. If the illusion does involve misperceived depth, manipulating the depth cue should change the illusion magnitude. Your task here is to decide whether the top line is longer than the bottom line.

RESULTS & DISCUSSION

1. Report your data for each condition. Did the illusion magnitude vary as the length of the arrowheads changed? Did it increase or decrease?

2. Do your results support the inappropriate size-distance (depth) scaling theory of the Muller-Lyer Illusion? Why or why not?

3. Why do you think the two illusion figures were offset when presented and presented for only a few seconds? Is this a good idea?

Measuring Illusions, continued
Vertical-Horizontal Illusion

One view of the vertical-horizontal illusion suggests that the bisection of the horizontal line by the vertical line in the standard illusion figure is the primary cause of the illusion. In this experiment you will be able to test this theory. The TOP condition presents the vertical line above and separate from the horizontal line. The BOTTOM condition presents the vertical line in the standard position, bisecting the horizontal line. Your task is to respond whether the vertical line is longer than the horizontal line. Be sure to wait until the response buttons are activated before you respond, and be ready for the briefly presented stimuli. Print out and save your data for each condition.

RESULTS & DISCUSSION

1. Report your data for each presentation condition. Was the illusion magnitude larger or smaller when the vertical line was not touching the horizontal line? (You have not performed the necessary statistics to allow a scientific conclusion concerning significance, but for these purposes, make a judgment based on your honest impressions.)

2. Does this support the theory that the bisection of the line is critical to the illusion, and not some difference in judging vertical and horizontal lines? If it does support that theory, is the data conclusive?

3. Have you noticed any strengths or problems associated with the method of limits?

Measuring Illusions, continued
Simultaneous Contrast

Simultaneous brightness contrast occurs when a test stimulus' brightness is influenced by the brightness of its background. Typically, test stimuli that are presented surrounded by a very dark background look brighter than when they are presented on a brighter background. One theory of contrast is based on the concept of lateral inhibition. That is, the lateral inhibition affecting the test stimulus is greater for brighter backgrounds than for darker backgrounds. As inhibition increases, the perceived brightness of the test stimulus decreases. If lateral inhibition is important, then the size of the test stimulus should influence the magnitude of the contrast effect. Smaller stimuli might be expected to show a greater contrast effect than larger stimuli. This experiment will allow you to manipulate test stimulus size and evaluate this theory.

Collect data for each of the test sizes. Your task is to decide whether the test circle on the right is brighter than the test circle on the left. Remember that the stimuli are presented briefly and that your response will not register unless the response buttons show bold type (highlighted). Save your data for each condition.

RESULTS & DISCUSSION

1. Report your data for each of the three stimulus sizes. Did the contrast effect change as stimulus size changed? (Ignore the fact that you have not performed any statistical tests. Give your general impression of the data.)

2. Does your data support the idea that lateral inhibition causes brightness contrast? Support your answer. Is any other data needed to be sure?

3. What is a PSE? How is it obtained using the method of limits? How could you find the difference threshold using your raw data?

Simultaneous Contrast: Dynamic

The appearance of a stimulus depends on not only its own characteristics, but also the background's characteristics. For example, stimuli that appear on a dark background tend to look lighter than when they appear on a light background. This variation of lightness in different contexts is known as lightness (or brightness) contrast. Some simultaneous contrast has been explained in terms of lateral inhibition. That is, activity in one neuron causes the inhibition of neurons adjacent to it. However, the standard concept of lateral inhibition in the retina cannot account for all simultaneous contrast phenomena.

This lab illustrates dynamic (involving change) simultaneous contrast. Note the change in lightness of the central circle as the background changes. To prove that the circle does not really change in lightness, click on WHITE (OR BLACK) and view the circle on a uniform background.

RESULTS & DISCUSSION

1. Report what you perceived in this demonstration.

2. What factors other than lateral inhibition might account for contrast effects like this?

Simultaneous Contrast: Static

The appearance of a stimulus depends on not only its own characteristics, but also the background's characteristics. For example, stimuli that appear on a dark background tend to look lighter than when they appear on a light background. This variation of lightness in different contexts is known as lightness (or brightness) contrast. Some simultaneous contrast has been explained in terms of lateral inhibition. That is, activity in one neuron causes the inhibition of neurons adjacent to it. However, the standard concept of lateral inhibition in the retina cannot account for all simultaneous contrast phenomena.

This lab illustrates static (steady-state) simultaneous contrast. Compare the lightness of the central circle on the two different backgrounds. To prove to yourself that they are actually the same lightness, view the central circles through two small holes in a piece of paper so that the background is the same for both circles.

RESULTS & DISCUSSION

1. Report what you perceived in this demonstration.

2. Why isn't lateral inhibition an adequate explanation for this kind of contrast effect?

Red-Green Opponent Cells

Hering proposed his opponent process theory long before there was physiological evidence for cells with color opponent characteristics. He based his theory on observations of color phenomena, and inferred such cells must exist. With the development of single-cell recording techniques, direct evidence of opponent cells became a reality. Single-cell recordings found that some cells made an excitatory response to long wavelength (red) light, but an inhibitory response to middle wavelength (green) light. Other cells showed this pattern for mid-long wavelength (yellow) and short (blue) wavelength light. These are the red-green and blue-yellow opponent cells, respectively. Interestingly, some red-green and yellow-blue opponent cells show the opposite pattern, with inhibitory responses to red and yellow and excitatory responses to green and blue.

In this exercise you will vary the intensity of red and green light stimulating a red-green cell. Begin with only the red light on, and note how the response rate changes as you adjust the intensity of the light. Turn that light off, and repeat with the green light. Finally, turn on both lights and adjust each light's intensity, again, observing the effect on the firing rate of the cell. The bar that represents the cells firing rate also changes color to represent the color that cell's output would indicate (ignoring any input from the other opponent system). Pay attention to the firing rate associated with red, with green, and with a black bar.

RESULTS & DISCUSSION

1. Report the cell's response to only red and only green light as intensity varied. How did these responses relate to the baseline firing rate of the cell?

2. Explain how the cell's response varied when both red and green lights were on and the intensity of each color light was manipulated. When did the cell signal red? Green? No color (black)?

3. As the "rainbow" created when sunlight is passed through a prism demonstrates, approximately colorless sunlight actually contains all the wavelengths of light that compose the visible spectrum. It contains light of short wavelengths corresponding to the color blue, long wavelengths corresponding to red, and everything in between. Based on what you have learned about the opponent cells, explain why sunlight appears colorless.

Missing Blue-Yellow Channel

When the blue-yellow opponent system is abnormal because of the absence of the short wavelength cone photopigment, tritanopia results. Tritanopes perceive all wavelengths as blue, grey (neutral) or red. The fact that they still perceive blue, rather than green, is not expected, and indicates that the blue-yellow system is not completely disabled in tritanopia. Whatever the specific explanation for this, tritanopes see blues up to their neutral point at 570 nm and reds at wavelengths above that.

This exercise asks you to predict the colors that are most likely to be confused by a tritanope. Knowing the wavelength that produces each of these colors will be helpful, so you might want to consult one of the previous color exercises or the textbook. If you are correct in a choice, a check mark will appear.

RESULTS & DISCUSSION

1. Which three tags are most likely to be confused by a tritanope? Why would these be confused?

2. Would the other two colors be confused? Why or why not?

Mixing Complimentary Colors

One of the aspects of color that proved difficult for trichromatic theory to explain fully is the phenomenon of complementary colors. Complementary colors are pairs of colors that produce an achromatic (grey) perception, rather than a third color, when they are mixed in equal quantities. Red-green and blue-yellow are two of the pairs of complementary colors. These colors are also linked in other color phenomena, and as a result, they were influential in the formulation of Hering's opponent-process theory of color vision.

This exercise simulates the mixture of two complementary colors. You should move the cursor along the line to vary the percentage of blue versus yellow light in the mixture. Notice how the color of the man's sweater changes as the mixture shifts from heavily blue to heavily yellow. Watch for the sweater to lose its color and look grey, and note where the cursor is located. Click on red-green to try the same exercise with those colors. This time, notice how the woman's sweater changes color.

RESULTS & DISCUSSION

1. Describe how the color of the sweater changed as the blue-yellow mixture varied. Where was the cursor when the sweater turned grey? Did the same thing occur for the red-green mixture?

2. Based on the color wheel represented in this exercise, what may we conclude about the relationship of complementary colors on the color wheel? What do you think the complementary color of the light blue-green color should be?

3. Explain why mixing complementary colors results in grey, according to the opponent process theory. Use either red-green or blue-yellow complementary pairs in your answer.

Strength of Blue-Yellow Mechanisms

Think back to the material on the spectral sensitivity curves for cones. Each type of cone responds to a particular range of wavelengths of light, with some wavelengths producing greater responses than others. Because of this, the strength of the input from the receptors to the opponent cells will vary depending on the wavelength of light that is present, and that will impact the strength of the output from the opponent cell.

This lab plots the relative output of a blue-yellow opponent cell as a function of wavelength. As you move the cursor across the color spectrum you will see three representations of the strength of response at each wavelength. First, the corresponding point in the plotted function for relative response will be marked. Second, a bar graph will show response intensity and the signaled color. Third, a numerical representation of the output will be shown in the small box.

Pay attention to the strength of the output as wavelength changes. Note when the cell's output changes from one color to the other and also where it gives no response. Note that the relative response function includes only positive values. The fact that the cell's response will be an inhibitory response for some wavelengths is not reflected in the plot. The absolute value of the response is used.

RESULTS & DISCUSSION

1. Approximately which wavelength produced the strongest response by the blue mechanism? By the yellow mechanism? Where was there no response by either mechanism?

2. Was there any wavelength that generated a response for both the blue and the yellow mechanism at the same time? Does this follow the predictions of the opponent-process theory? Why?

3. The maximum response strength is not the same for both the blue and the yellow mechanisms. Is this important? Why or why not?

Strength of Red-Green Mechanism

This lab is the same as the previous lab, except that the red-green mechanism is illustrated.

Again, as you drag the cursor across the spectrum, the relative strength of the response is represented as a plotted function, a bar graph, and a numerical value. As before, all values are positive; the absolute value of inhibitory responses are used. Pay attention to the strength of the response as wavelength changes. Note the wavelengths where each mechanism's response is maximal, and also where no response occurs.

RESULTS & DISCUSSION

1. Approximately which wavelength generates the maximum response in the red mechanism? In the green mechanism? When does no response occur in the red mechanism? In the green mechanism? In neither mechanism?

2. Why does the opponent cell produce no response to certain wavelengths?

3. The relative strength of the response in the red-green mechanism is not unique for each wavelength. For example, the relative response at both 500 nm and approximately 540 nm (which is near the green-yellow border) is 71. Why do these wavelengths differ if the output of the red-green mechanism is the same?

Opponent-Process Coding of Hue

The opponent process theory of color vision states that the relative activity of two opponent systems, blue-yellow and red-green, is used to determine the hue of a stimulus. The response of each opponent system can be either inhibitory, signaling one range of wavelengths (e.g., middle to long wavelengths), or excitatory, signaling the other range of wavelengths (e.g., short wavelengths), and the strength of response will vary by wavelength. The profile of responses from the two opponent systems will differ for each wavelength.

This demonstration illustrates the response profiles of the opponent systems as stimulus wavelength is varied. Information from previous exercises is presented simultaneously for easier comparison. Move the cursor across the spectrum and note the output of each system. Pay attention to the changes that occur when small adjustments in wavelength are made.

RESULTS & DISCUSSION

1. Report and compare the responses of the two opponent systems for a wavelength in the blue region, green region, yellow region, and red region.

2. Are there any wavelengths at which only one opponent system produces a response? Explain why or why not.

Troxler Effect

The Troxler effect, which dates back to 1804, is the fading or suppression of images that are stabilized on the retina. That is, when an image remains in exactly the same location, adaptation causes that information to be lost. Any movement, however, produces new input and the image is once again perceived. The constant small movements of our eyes, even when fixating on a point, prevents the Troxler effect in most conditions. One exception, however, is when the peripheral image contains no distinct contours.

This demonstration allows you to experience the Troxler effect. You should stare at the small dot in the fuzzy contour figure. Do not move your eyes at all. Observe what happens to the fuzzy border and circular region of the stimulus. If you have trouble when you use two eyes, try viewing the stimulus with only one eye. Try the same thing with the sharp border figure.

RESULTS & DISCUSSION

1. Describe what you perceived in each stimulus condition. Did the border and circular area disappear?

2. Why doesn't the Troxler effect occur when there is a sharp border? After all, you were staring just as steadily, so the image should have been as stabilized in that condition as in the fuzzy border condition. (Hint: Remember that your eyes are not absolutely still.)

Chapter 8: Perceiving Depth and Size

Virtual Labs for Chapter 8:

Convergence as a Depth Cue
Convergence
Shape from Shading - Shadows
Motion Parallax
The Horopter and Corresponding Points
Disparity and Retinal Location
Pictures
Outlines
Depth Perception
Random-Dot Stereogram
The Muller-Lyer Illusion
The Muller-Lyer Illusion 2
The Muller-Lyer Variations
Ponzo Illusion
Size Perception and Depth
Horizontal-Vertical Illusion
Poggendorf Illusion
Zollner Illusion

Convergence as a Depth Cue

The general categories of depth cues include monocular pictorial and movement cues, binocular disparity, and oculomotor cues. The term *oculomotor* refers to eye (oculo) muscles or movement (motor). It also can refer to eye position. There are two oculomotor cues for depth: convergence and accommodation.

Convergence refers to the position of the two eyes when looking at some object. The two eyes must turn inward more and more to fixate on the object as the object gets closer and closer. This causes the muscles on the outer side of the eyes to be stretched more and more, and the muscles on the inner side to have to contract more and more intensely. This information is transmitted from the eye muscles to the brain, providing information about the eyes' positions. Thus, the angle of convergence of the eyes may be used as a cue for the location (depth) of the object.

This lab allows you to see how eye position is related to the depth (distance) of the object being viewed. Move the object closer and note how the angle of convergence changes. Compare convergence for small and large distances.

RESULTS & DISCUSSION

1. Draw a diagram to illustrate what is meant by the convergence angle of the eyes. How does the convergence angle change as an object moves farther away from the observer?

2. When will convergence be most useful as a depth cue? Why?

Convergence

Convergence is the movement of the two eyes necessary to focus on an object in the environment. To focus on a close object, the eyes must converge more than when they focus on a distant object. Information about eye position, then, may be used as a cue for spatial relations. Because eye movements are involved, convergence is one of the oculomotor cues for spatial relations.

In this exercise you will see how convergence operates and may be used in perceiving spatial relationships.

RESULTS & DISCUSSION

1. What two things must be known in order to use convergence information to compute the distance of an object in the environment? Explain why this information is required.

2. What is vergence angle? How does it relate to convergence, and what is the relationship of vergence angle and distance?

3. When will convergence lose its effectiveness as a distance cue? Why?

Shape from Shading - Shadows

The amount of light reflected by different regions of an object can provide important information about the object's shape. Areas that are not directly facing the light source are not as strongly illuminated and appear darker than other areas. Thus, shadows provide information about the surface characteristics of objects.

In this exercise you will observe the effect shadows may have in three-dimensional perception of a form. Pay attention to how the form appears both before and after motion begins, and when all surfaces are equally illuminated.

RESULTS & DISCUSSION

1. Describe the appearance of the object and the nature of illumination in the first part of the demonstration. What role did shadows play in your perception of the object?

2. Did the object appear different when moving? If so, how?

3. What happened when all surfaces were equally illuminated? Explain why this occurred.

Motion Parallax

As you've learned from previous demonstrations, motion often provides rich information that influences perception. In addition to assisting in form perception, motion contributes to depth or distance perception. As an observer moves through the environment, the images of objects in the environment move at different speeds and in different directions depending on their position relative to the observer's point of fixation. This is called motion parallax.

This exercise demonstrates motion parallax. Pay attention to the initial location of the three people in the scene, and note how their positions shift as the camera (observer) moves across the room.

RESULTS & DISCUSSION

1. Describe how the positions of the three people changed relative to the position of the observer. Explain why this occurs.

2. Motion parallax involves differences in the speed of position changes, too. Why does this occur, and how is it related to distance?

3. What other movement-produced cues for depth occurred in this demonstration?

The Horopter and Corresponding Points

To understand the binocular depth cue retinal (or binocular) disparity requires that you understand what is meant by corresponding points and horopter. The concept of corresponding points arises because the two eyes are separated in space, and this means that the image of an object will not always fall in exactly the same position (on corresponding points) is both eyes. As you will see in another lab, this retinal position information is critical to a very important cue for depth, binocular disparity.

The horopter is a curved plane in space that passes through the point of fixation and on which all points at a given level will be equidistant from the observer. The images of objects that are located on the horopter will always fall on corresponding points, so the horopter will be a critical reference point for descriptions of an object's spatial position and descriptions of binocular disparity.

In this exercise you will explore the relationship of objects on the horopter and the retinal position of objects located on and off the horopter. First, make sure you understand the concept of corresponding points, and then proceed to the demonstration about the horopter. Make sure you understand how changes in the position of the horopter relate to convergence, and how changes in location along the horopter affect retinal position of the image in each eye.

RESULTS & DISCUSSION

1. What is meant when an image is said to fall on corresponding points? How is the concept of corresponding points related to the concept of the horopter?

2. As the horopter moves farther from the observer, how does convergence change? If you move an object to a different point along one horopter, how will convergence change?

3. If images in the two eyes fall on corresponding points when the object is in its original position, will the images still fall on corresponding points when the object moves to a new location along the horopter? What if the object is moved to a position off the horopter?

Disparity and Retinal Location

When two objects are located at different distances from the observer, one will not be on the horopter, and thus, the image for that object will not fall on corresponding points in the two eyes. That is, disparity will occur. The difference in the distances of the two objects is critical in determining the amount of retinal disparity present, and whether the second object is in front of or behind the horopter determines the exact form of disparity (i.e., crossed vs. uncrossed) that occurs. This means that retinal disparity can be used as a cue for depth. Because disparity requires two eyes, it is considered a binocular depth cue.

When disparity is the only depth cue available, it still can produce a remarkable perception of three dimensions. Those random dot, or "Magic Eye," posters that suddenly reveal a realistic three-dimensional perception when viewed correctly are based on retinal disparity. In fact, the visual system seems especially prepared to use disparity information to build a three-dimensional perception. Some brain cells respond maximally only when disparity is present.

This exercise demonstrates how retinal disparity operates. As you change the spatial position of the sphere, pay close attention to where its image falls in each eye. Make sure you understand why the images are said to be on non-corresponding points.

RESULTS & DISCUSSION

1. When the sphere moved off the horopter, its image no longer fell on corresponding points. Explain why these are called non-corresponding points. How is their position different in the two eyes?

2. As the sphere moved closer, how did disparity change?

3. Describe the relationship between disparity and spatial position. Identify and explain two different types of disparity (see your text).

Pictures

As a child, did you have a toy into which you looked and saw rich three-dimensional pictures of cartoons, or Disney World, or exotic locations? Stereograms, pairs of pictures that create retinal disparity when viewed properly, have been popular for the past century. Your toy isolated the picture each of your eyes saw by having you look through two different openings. The picture each eye received was taken from a slightly different position so that retinal disparity is produced when viewed.

Another technique is to print two stimuli in different colors and in slightly different positions and to use colored filters to allow each eye to see only one of the two images. The filter masks the image printed in the corresponding color, so each eye sees only the image printed in the other color. The different positions produce retinal disparity and stereopsis.

View the pictures with the red-green glasses and note what you see. Reverse the glasses and observe how your perception changes.

RESULTS & DISCUSSION

1. Describe what you saw when you viewed the pictures with the red-green glasses.

2. What happened when you reversed the glasses? When did the position of the glasses make the most difference?

3. Explain why reversing the glasses changed your perception.

Outlines

The technique for producing stereopsis used in the **Pictures** lab is used again here. However, the stimuli will be line drawings and you will be able to manipulate the amount of retinal disparity. Before viewing the stimuli with the red-green glasses, manipulate disparity and observe how the red and green outlines change in relation to each other. With the glasses on, again manipulate disparity, and pay attention to how different amounts of disparity influence the depth perceived. Be sure to check to see if the Necker cube reverses as it does in the two-dimensional versions.

RESULTS & DISCUSSION

1. As you increased disparity, how did the stimulus change (viewed without the glasses)? How did your perception change?

2. How did disparity relate to the depth perceived when the stimuli were viewed with the glasses?

3. Did the Necker cube reverse orientations? Why is this to be expected?

Depth Perception

Retinal disparity is a powerful cue for depth. Stereograms can include no depth cues other than disparity, yet the perception of depth is quite strong. Generally, as disparity increases, so too does perceived depth. The object's position relative to the horopter is determined by whether the disparity is crossed or uncrossed. Uncrossed disparity makes the object appear beyond the horopter, and crossed disparity makes the object appear in front of the horopter. So, as uncrossed disparity increases, the object moves farther away from the observer. As crossed disparity increases, the object moves closer to the observer.

There are limits to the usefulness of disparity, however. When disparity becomes too great, the brain cannot fuse the images, and diplopia (double vision) occurs. This causes depth perception to become inaccurate. The range of disparities that do lead to fusion and accurate depth perception are in Panum's area. This is a region that extends some distance in front of and behind the horopter.

In this experiment you will make depth judgments using a magnitude estimation procedure. A standard stimulus given a rating of 100 appears to the left of fixation, and a comparison stimulus appears to the right. Rate the depth of the comparison stimulus relative to the standard. Red-green filter glasses are necessary to experience depth perception because disparity is manipulated in stereograms. In one condition all disparities will be crossed, and in the other they will be uncrossed. When the disparity is beyond Panum's area, you will see a double image, but you will experience some perception of depth. Give a rating, but add a D to indicate diplopia (e.g., 150D).

RESULTS & DISCUSSION

1. Supply a print-out of your data. How did your depth ratings relate to disparity?

2. What disparities produced diplopia (where does Panum's fusional area terminate)? Is depth perception possible outside of Panum's area? Why or why not? What is the significance of this?

3. Were your ratings for crossed and uncrossed disparities very similar, or did the functions differ? What does this suggest?

Random dot stereograms produce a vivid three-dimensional perception using only the depth cue of retinal disparity. The anaglyphs shown here are actually composed of two superimposed arrays of dots, with each array shown in a different color. The different colors, combined with the red-green filter glasses, cause one array to be seen by only the right eye, and the other only by the left eye. Retinal disparity is introduced by shifting a region of the dots slightly to one side in one of the arrays. Thus, the right eye receives a slightly different image than does the left eye. Although the ability to perceive depth based on only one type of information is surprising, perhaps more surprising is the fact that complex objects can be perceived when the images of the two eyes are combined by the brain, even though each image is composed only of random dots, rather than organized contours!

This lab allows you to manipulate the level of disparity between the two images, the dot density (how much information is contained in each array), and the size of the object. Vary the disparity and note how the depth changes. As you manipulate dot density, pay attention to the density required to perceive the object and depth, and compare this across the different patterns. Also vary object size to evaluate the importance of this variable.

RESULTS & DISCUSSION

1. When you decreased the level of disparity, how did your perception of the object change? How little disparity was needed to produce a 3D perception?

2. Did reducing dot density prevent a 3D view? Was the impact of reduced density about the same for all the figures?

3. Did object size influence your ability to perceive depth in the picture?

The Muller-Lyer Illusion

The Muller-Lyer illusion is one of the most well-known geometric illusions. In the Muller-Lyer illusion, the length of a line is misperceived because of the context in which the line occurs. The line has different forms at each end, and these forms significantly influence the appearance of the line.

Several theories have been proposed to explain the Mueller-Lyer illusion. One of the most common theories is Gregory's misapplied size constancy scaling view. This theory proposes the Muller-Lyer figure is perceived as a three-dimensional figure, rather two-dimensional, because of pictorial depth cues that are present. Because three dimensions are assumed, the size constancy mechanism becomes involved, inappropriately, and an incorrect size-distance scaling occurs and produces the illusion.

In this lab you will make line length judgments for the Muller-Lyer stimulus. Move the cursor until the two lines look the same length. Complete 5 trials and record the mean illusion estimate. After working with one version of the illusion, complete 5 trials with the other version. Note how your length estimates compare to the first version of the illusion.

RESULTS & DISCUSSION

1. Report the mean illusion value for each version of the Muller-Lyer figure. How did your perception of line length differ in the two versions?

2. Give a brief explanation of the Muller-Lyer illusion using the misperceived depth viewpoint.

3. What is the depth cue that is present in the illusion figure?

The Muller-Lyer illusion is one of the most famous illusions of size. Lines that are equal length appear to be shorter or longer depending on the forms that appear at the ends of the lines. One of the most commonly cited theories of this illusion, and many other illusions of size, is based on the idea that depth cues produce an inappropriate perception of three dimensions, activating the size constancy mechanism, and that this leads to a misperception of length.

In this demonstration you will view the standard version of the Muller-Lyer illusion figure. Judge whether the two horizontal lines appear to be equal in length. Also try rotating your head sideways and viewing the illusion figure from that position. To view the actual length of the lines, remove the end pieces of the figures.

RESULTS & DISCUSSION

1. Explain why misperceived depth might account for this illusion. Which depth cue is dominant in this figure?

2. If you rotate your head sideways and view the illusion figure from that position, does the illusion still occur? Would a misperceived depth explanation still be appropriate? Why or why not?

The Muller-Lyer Variations

Although the "arrowhead" version of the Muller-Lyer illusion is the most common, there are several variations that have been the subject of research. Most of these variations have been produced to test specific theories of the Muller-Lyer illusion. For example, variations that reduce or eliminate depth cues have been used to prove that the depth-based theories are not completely adequate explanations of the illusion. Some researchers argue that all variations must be explained by a single theory. Other researchers, however, argue that the variations might best be considered different illusions and that one general theory is not appropriate.

In this lab you will view three common variations of the Muller-Lyer illusion. As before, judge the length of the horizontal lines and decide if they are equal. Pay attention to the strength of any illusion observed in the three figures.

RESULTS & DISCUSSION

1. Does the illusion seem approximately the same strength in all three variants? What does this suggest about the origin of the illusion?

2. What do you think each of these variations was designed to test?

3. Can the traditional depth-based theory explain all three variants? Explain.

Ponzo Illusion

The Ponzo illusion is one of several illusions that involve misperception of size or length. Two lines appear between lines that converge toward the "horizon" or the top of the visual field. The same general explanation given for the Muller-Lyer illusion is often given for the Ponzo illusion. This explanation states the illusion is based on a misperception of depth, leading to inappropriate size-distance scaling, and thus, misperceived line length or stimulus size.

The Ponzo illusion has appeared in many variations. The simplest has two converging lines "pointed" toward the top of a blank field, with two horizontal lines of equal length between the converging lines. The basic figure is sometimes rotated, and the lines to be judged are sometimes replaced by circles. Sometimes details are added to provide a context that resembles the real environment, as in the version shown in this exercise.

This exercise allows you to collect measurements of the illusion's strength. Adjust the two lines until they appear equal in length. Complete several trials and record your results. To see that you are misjudging length, remove the converging lines and background after adjusting the lines, and see if the lines look equal in that context.

FOLLOW-UP

1. Report your data. Did the lines look equal when they were shown in isolation?

2. What depth cues are present in the Ponzo figure shown in this exercise? What do you think would happen to the illusion if the depth cues were increased? Decreased?

3. Using the inappropriate size-distance scaling theory, explain the Ponzo illusion.

Size Perception and Depth

Although many geometric illusions use simple forms such as circles or lines, more complex forms produce the same illusions. Here, two monsters are shown on a background that suggests depth, and once again, the monster nearer the bottom of the field appears smaller than the monster higher up.

To prove that the two monsters actually are the same size, drag the lower, "smaller," monster up to overlap the other monster. Identify the depth cues that are thought to produce the illusion.

RESULTS & DISCUSSION

1. What aspects of the scene suggest depth, rather than a flat picture?

2. Why isn't accurate information about the size of an object's image on the retina adequate for maintaining size constancy?

3. If the image presented in this exercise really was a three-dimensional scene, would size constancy occur? Explain your answer.

Horizontal-Vertical Illusion

Among the oldest and strongest illusions studied in psychology is the horizontal-vertical illusion. It was formally described by Wundt in 1868, and although it has been the subject of many experiments, a completely adequate explanation is not available. In the horizontal-vertical illusion, the vertical line in an upside-down T is perceived to be significantly longer than the horizontal line, even though they are equal in length. The illusion also occurs with other arrangements of the horizontal and vertical lines.

This exercise requires you to adjust the horizontal line segment until it appears to be the same length as the vertical segment. Click on RESULT to see a numerical comparison of the two lines' actual lengths, and then on COMPARE to see the two lines side by side for a visual comparison. Complete 10 trials, noting the magnitude of the illusion on each trial.

RESULTS & DISCUSSION

1. Report your results for each trial and also your mean error. Did you ever show no illusion?

2. For some illusions, illusion magnitude diminishes with practice. Does your data show a practice effect? Why might such an effect occur?

3. Why do you think the vertical-horizontal illusion occurs? How might you test your idea?

Poggendorf Illusion

In the Poggendorf illusion, line segments intersect two vertical lines (or other figure) at an angle. When the two line segments are aligned so that they could represent one continuous straight line, they do not appear to be aligned. One line appears higher than the other.

As with other illusions, several theories have been proposed. One commonly cited theory suggests that the angles is misperceived because acute angles tend to be overestimated and obtuse angles tend to be underestimated. Another theory states that the figure is perceived as a 3-dimensional figure in which the two lines are on two different receding planes that form a right angle with the rectangle. Distorted perspective due in part to angle over- and under-estimation leads to the illusion. However, neither of these theories can account for all of the variants of the illusion.

This demonstration presents the standard Poggendorf illusion figure. Judge whether the two line segments are aligned to represent one continuous line. To check the alignment without the influence of the vertical lines, click on DELETE RECTANGLE.

RESULTS & DISCUSSION

1. Did the two lines look properly aligned? If not, how would you have adjusted the line on the right side?

2. Some researchers have noted that this illusion resembles a partial Muller-Lyer figure (note the angles created by the intersections of the lines). Use this idea to explain the Poggendorf illusion.

Zollner Illusion

The Zollner illusion dates back to the mid-1800s. In the Zollner illusion, parallel lines appear to converge, apparently due to the transversals, short intersecting lines, located down the length of each parallel line. As with other illusions, several factors have been suggested as possible influences on the illusion, including inaccuracy in angle perception and the influence of a three-dimensional perception, but a definitive explanation is not universally accepted. As you view the illusion, try to identify factors that you think might cause the illusion.

This lab allows you to alter the illusion figure to explore the conditions that produce the illusion. By clicking on the buttons you can remove and replace various components of the illusion figure. Make sure you examine the full illusion figure (the first view) and all of the following modifications: (1) vertical transversals on diagonals and horizontal transversals without diagonals; (2) transversals only (look for the illusion in the illusory contours of the diagonals); (3) horizontal transversals on diagonals and vertical transversals without diagonals; (4) three diagonals only; and (5) all diagonals only. Consider what the illusion strength in these different conditions suggests about the illusion's origin.

RESULTS & DISCUSSION

1. Report the strength of the illusion in all the viewing conditions.

2. In which conditions did perception of depth occur, and how does this relate to illusion magnitude?

3. Was the illusion present for the illusory contour diagonals (Condition 2)? What might this suggest?

4. Why do you think the illusion occurs? Justify your answer with data from this exercise.

Chapter 9: Perceiving Movement

Virtual Labs for Chapter 9:

The Phi Phenomenon, Space, and Time
Illusory Contour Motion
Apparent Movement and Figural Selection
Motion Capture
Induced Movement
The Waterfall Illusion
The Spiral Motion Aftereffect
Color Contingent Motion
Motion Contingent Color
Motion Parallax and Object Form
Kinetic Depth Effect
Shape From Movement
Form and Motion
Motion Reference
Corollary Discharge Model
Biological Motion
Motion and Introduced Occlusion
Field Effects and Apparent Movement
Context and Apparent Speed
Motion in Depth

The Phi Phenomenon, Space, and Time

The phi phenomenon is a type of apparent movement. Two stimuli are presented separated both spatially and in time. Rather than seeing two stimuli, however, one moving stimulus is perceived. The phi stimulus partially mimics what occurs on the retina when an object is moving. That is, different locations on the retina are stimulated at different times. So, it isn't too surprising that movement is seen when no real movement occurs.

It is important to remember that phi movement isn't always seen with two alternating stimuli. The two stimuli's intensity, physical separation, and separation in time must be in the proper relationship for a strong perception of movement to occur. Korte's Law is a mathematical representation of this relationship and is used to produce optimal phi movement.

In this exercise you will examine the relationship between spatial separation and the interstimulus interval required for phi movement to be perceived. Adjust the interstimulus interval (the speed of alternation) until your perception is of one sphere moving across the field, rather than two spheres being illuminated at different locations. Be sure to set the physical separation at 10, 20, 30, 40, 50 and 60 units and find the interstimulus interval that produces strong phi movement at each. Also note what happens when the interval is at its lowest and highest.

RESULTS & DISCUSSION

1. Report your findings for the 6 separation settings. What general relationship is apparent?

2. What brain mechanism might account for the phi phenomenon and the importance of the magnitude of the separation in time and space?

3. Strobe lights are bright lights that flash on and off, illuminating the scene for a brief moment. They commonly are used in dance clubs or parties for special effect. Explain why a dancer's movement appears very choppy and disconnected, or even that the person has magically changed location, when the interflash interval is long.

Illusory Contour Motion

When the forms in a stimulus array suggest the possible presence of an additional, occluding form, an illusory version of that form may be perceived. The edges of the form are called illusory contours, and they typically bound an area of different apparent brightness than the rest of the array. Of course, no actual brightness differences occur. Illusory contours have been important in the discussion of perceptual organization and form perception.

In this exercise, you will see a sine wave grating in motion. A black bar separates the upper and lower sections of the array. Look for the illusory contours of the grating. Before beginning, click the **?** (Help) to see some additional information about this phenomenon.

RESULTS & DISCUSSION

1. Describe the illusory contours and the conditions in which they appeared.

2. Why do you think motion was important? What Gestalt principle might be responsible?

285

Apparent Movement and Figural Selection

Apparent movement doesn't occur equally for all stimuli. Specific characteristics are very important for determining whether apparent movement will occur, and how that movement will appear. The specific pattern of apparent movement will depend on rules that mimic how objects move in the environment.

This demonstration illustrates how the specific attributes of the stimuli influence the pattern of movement perceived. As the instructions suggest, begin by examining the basic stimuli used to produce both the split and figural selection conditions. Knowing what the stimuli in the two inducing frames are like is very important to understanding the significance of the movement perceived. After you have examined the stimuli, click on START to initiate the presentation of the split movement condition. Adjust the interstimulus interval as needed to produce a strong apparent movement effect. Notice the nature of the apparent movement in this condition.

Next click FIGURAL SELECTION to initiate the second type of movement. Pay attention to the characteristics of the movement. Vary the separation of the stimuli in the second frame relative to the stimulus in the first frame. Note whether the movement changes as the second stimulus is manipulated.

RESULTS & DISCUSSION

1. What type of movement occurred in the split condition? Why does it make sense for this to occur?

2. What type of movement occurred in the figural selection condition? What happened when the distance between the stimuli was adjusted? What rule seems to govern where motion is perceived?

3. What do you think would happen if the two bars in the split condition were located different distances from the initial stimulus?

287

Motion Capture

Motion can help object recognition, and motion can influence perceptual organization. In motion capture, smaller components are grouped together and move with a moving object. The moving object "captures" other components and causes them to appear to move, also.

You will observe motion capture in this exercise. In the basic display, a white square will appear to move from one panel to another. In reality, the four spheres in each panel will change to four partial spheres, and this will create an illusory contour figure of a square. Apparent movement will occur as this manipulation occurs in one panel and then the next. When dots are added to the background, the illusory square will "capture" the dots, making them appear part of the moving square.

Adjust the interstimulus interval until you get a strong perception of the illusory white square moving. After observing the basic figure, add the dots to the background and note whether they appear to move.

RESULTS & DISCUSSION

1. What happened when you added the dots to the background?

2. Why do you think motion capture occurs?

Induced Movement

Like apparent movement, induced movement is an illusion that a stimulus is moving, when it really isn't. Unlike apparent movement, induced movement does involve a stimulus that actually moves. It is the movement of that stimulus that causes, induces, the perception that another object is moving. That is, a moving context can produce the illusion that a stable object is moving.

Perhaps you have experienced this effect when having your car washed in an automatic car wash. Although the spray mechanism moves along the unmoving car, it is common for the driver to feel that the car is moving – sometimes strongly enough to cause a quick braking response. The view of movement of a structure outside the car and the water stream across the windows mimics the situation when the car is moving in the rain. Especially interesting in this situation is that induced motion is experienced both visually and in terms of felt body position!

In this exercise you will see induced movement in another familiar context. Moving clouds will cause a motionless figure to appear to move. Be sure to reverse the direction of motion and observe how the induced motion changes. Begin this demonstration with a restricted view. View the demonstration through a hole in a piece of paper or a paper tube so that the display's frame is not visible. Next, view the demonstration without a restricted view. Be sure to note any difference in the induced motion effect.

RESULTS & DISCUSSION

1. When you restricted your field of view, did the object appear to move? How did the object move relative to the moving clouds?

2. Compare the induced motion perceived in the two different viewing conditions. Why do you think the effects differed?

3. What factors do you think determine whether induced motion will occur? Why do we experience induced motion in a car wash, for example, but not when a person walks by our parked car?

The Waterfall Illusion

The waterfall illusion is an example of a motion aftereffect. When an observer views a series of horizontal lines moving downward, an aftereffect will follow in which movement is seen in stable objects. This illusion's name refers to the similarity of the stimulus display to the cascade of a waterfall. In fact, staring at a waterfall and then looking at an unmoving part of the scene produces the same effect.

In this demonstration you will explore interesting aspects of the waterfall illusion. To begin, select a middle range speed. Click START to initiate movement. Position your cursor over STOP so that you can turn the display off later without having to shift your gaze away from the display. At the end of the minute, click STOP and keep looking at the display. Note whether you perceive any movement and its direction and speed. Reportedly, the illusion disappears if the moving bars and the stationary bars are perfectly aligned when the motion is halted. If this arrangement happens to occur as you work with the demonstration, be sure to note whether the illusion was still present under those conditions.

Repeat the exercise using a slower and a faster speed, and compare the resulting illusions. Reverse the direction of movement and repeat the exercise at one speed. Also, rather than staring at the fixation point, track the moving lines, following one line at a time from top to bottom during the adaptation period. Wait until the aftereffect is gone, then view the display with one eye only, and use the other eye to check for any illusory movement. As you work with this demonstration, think about what the waterfall illusion suggests about the mechanisms underlying motion perception.

RESULTS & DISCUSSION

1. What did you see when you stopped the motion of the display? How did the illusion relate to the original motion? Did the original speed influence the illusion? The direction? If you were lucky enough to have the bars in perfect alignment when stopped, did the illusion occur?

2. Did the waterfall illusion occur when you tracked the movement rather than staring at one point? Does the illusion occur when an un-adapted eye is used to check for the aftereffect?

3. Why do you think the waterfall illusion occurs? What does this demonstration suggest about the origin of the illusion in the nervous system (eye vs. brain)?

The Spiral Motion Aftereffect

The spiral motion aftereffect is very similar to the waterfall illusion, except in the nature of the motion perceived. Again, extensive exposure to movement in one direction results in illusory motion in a subsequent stable display. The spiral motion produces a perception of expansion or contraction, so the aftereffect can produce some surprising effects.

In this demonstration you will experience the spiral aftereffect and how it can influence a different, realistic figure. Put the spiral in motion and stare at the center for approximately 45 seconds. Note whether you perceive expansion or shrinking. After you are thoroughly adapted to the rotating spiral, stop the movement and continue looking at the spiral figure. Note the nature of the aftereffect.

Repeat the adaptation procedure, but instead of clicking on STOP, click on NOVEL STIMULUS. Pay attention to any changes that occur in your perception of that stimulus.

When you no longer detect any trace of the aftereffect, repeat the adaptation procedure once more, but close one eye this time. After adaptation, stop the motion and view the stationary spiral figure with the previously closed eye. Note whether the aftereffect occurs in the closed eye as well as in the adapted eye.

RESULTS & DISCUSSION

1. Describe the spiral motion aftereffect. How did the direction of the illusory motion compare to the motion in the spiral stimulus?

2. What happened when you viewed the novel stimulus? What does this tell us about the aftereffect?

3. Did interocular transfer of the illusion occur? (Did you see the illusion with the eye that you had closed during adaptation?) What does this suggest about the location of the illusion?

4. Use the concept of motion-sensitive cells to explain why this illusion occurs.

Color Contingent Motion

In some of the other demonstrations you have adapted with one eye and looked for aftereffects with the other. When the aftereffect is seen with an unadapted eye, the effect originates in the brain instead of in the eye. Also, the explanation given for most aftereffects refers to systems that rely on a comparison of the output of two channels of input that are each maximally responsive to specific stimulus characteristics.

In this lab two red/green gratings moving in opposite directions are presented above and below a small white fixation bar. After the adaptation period ends, one grating will be replaced by a blue/yellow grating and both gratings will stop moving. Continue looking at the white bar, but watch for any movement aftereffect. Pay particular attention to the strength and duration of the aftereffects. Note whether the motion aftereffect seen for the red/green grating is the same strength and duration as that seen for the blue/yellow grating.

RESULTS & DISCUSSION

1. Describe any aftereffect you observed in the test gratings, and compare this to the adaptation gratings.

2. Was the aftereffect equally strong and long-lasting with the red/green and blue/yellow gratings?

3. Is this effect surprising? Provide a possible explanation, and discuss what this aftereffect suggests about the color and motion systems.

Motion Contingent Color

The previous lab showed that motion aftereffects may be contingent upon the test stimulus being a particular color. This demonstration shows that color aftereffects may be contingent on a test stimulus that moves in a particular direction.

In this lab, two sine wave gratings are alternated during an adaptation period. One grating is red and the other is green. Note the direction each grating is moving. Look at the small white fixation bar that appears in the middle of the display. The adaptation period is quite long, but this is necessary for the aftereffect to be visible. When the adaptation period is complete, the colored gratings will be replaced by two identical grey gratings moving in opposite directions, one above the white bar and one below it. Keep looking at the white fixation bar during the test period. Look for any color that is visible in the two gratings.

RESULTS & DISCUSSION

1. Describe the aftereffect you experienced for the right-moving (top) and the left-moving (bottom) test stimulus gratings. How did the color relate to that of the adaptation stimulus?

2. This aftereffect reportedly is very long-lasting when adaptation is sufficient. Is this a potential problem for standard explanations of aftereffects? Why or why not?

Motion Parallax and Object Form

When an object is rotated, as in the kinetic depth effect, the object's form often will become unambiguous. A similar effect occurs when the observer moves through the environment and views the form from different perspectives. As the observer moves, the relationships between parts of the object become clear, and object perception is possible.

This demonstration illustrates how changing views of an object can assist object perception. Click on each location button to reveal a shadow view of the object from different locations. Try to identify the actual shape of the object. Begin by selecting the locations randomly, then repeat, viewing the locations in order. By clicking on SOLUTION, you'll see the illuminated object.

RESULTS & DISCUSSION

1. Why is object perception difficult when only a shadow view is available? What is missing? Is this a common situation in the real world?

2. Compare your ability to accurately perceive the object based on a single viewing condition. When multiple conditions were possible, did the order in which you viewed them influence your perception? Why?

Kinetic Depth Effect

The kinetic depth effect involves improved object perception when an object is put in motion. Most typically, a shadow of a three-dimensional object is cast on a screen, and an observer attempts to identify the object. In many cases the two-dimensional shadow provides only ambiguous or very incomplete information about the object, and the perception is two-dimensional. When the object is rotated, the previously unrecognizable object becomes easily recognized, and it is perceived as three-dimensional. Motion produces cues for depth that allow the three-dimensional perception, and that in turn, can assist in object recognition. The relationship of the parts of a complex stimulus become clear, and the object is perceptually organized and recognized.

In this exercise you will experience the kinetic depth effect for four different shapes. When viewed initially, their images are identical. When they are put in motion, however, note how the shape is easily recognized. Think about the kind of information that is provided when the shapes are put in motion and whether depth perception is involved. Click on each box to start that shape in motion.

RESULTS & DISCUSSION

1. Report the four shapes. Did rotation produce a perception of a solid, three-dimensional object?

2. Why did the shapes become easily recognizable when rotated? Was depth perception an important component? Explain.

Shape From Movement

When stimuli move in relation to one another, the observer may perceive not individually moving stimuli, but instead, moving objects. In this demonstration you will initially see an array of dots. As the demonstration proceeds, portions of the dot array will begin to move. Note what you perceive when the dots are in motion.

RESULTS & DISCUSSION

1. Describe what you observed when some of the dots in the array began to move.

2. Why does this effect occur? What does this tell us about the perceptual system?

3. What do you think a Gestalt psychologist would have to say about this effect?

Form and Motion

Motion conveys information that goes far beyond the motion itself. As the kinetic depth effect demonstrates, motion may also provide information that transforms an array of what appears to be random dots into a recognizable form. Motion may help with the perceptual segregation of figure and ground, and it may provide cues for depth and spatial relationships between objects or between objects and the observer.

Several variables influence the perception of form through motion. The amount of information about the stimulus that is present, the extent to which the motion of the stimulus elements are correlated, the presence of movement in other areas of the environment, and the speed of the movement may all influence the perception of form in movement.

This demonstration allows you to explore the impact of several variables on motion perception. Read the background information and instructions before beginning the demonstration. You should vary the correlation of the dots' motion, the shape of the object, the number of dots involved, speed, and several background variables. Manipulate these variables in a systematic way so that the following questions may be answered, and report your observations for each parameter setting you examine.

RESULTS & DISCUSSION

1. What correlation value is required for object identification? Does this vary significantly across different shapes?

2. Under what conditions does the background make object recognition more difficult?

3. Does the speed of motion influence object perception? Explain your answer.

Motion Reference

The nature of motion is not always determined by only the actual motion of an object. The relationship of the object's motion to other aspects of the stimulus array can be very important. Motion will sometimes conform to the patterns commonly seen in the real world, and thus, may be significantly influenced by the perceptual organization of the rest of the stimulus array.

In this exercise you will see three dots in motion. Two of the dots will move horizontally. Pay close attention to the way the third dot moves and its relationship to the other two dots. To see how the third dot is actually moving, click on HIDE REFERENCE DOTS. Compare the motion perceived with and without the reference (horizontal motion) dots.

RESULTS & DISCUSSION

1. How did the third (middle) dot appear to move when the reference dots were present? Without the reference dots?

2. What concept in motion perception does this represent?

3. What does this tell us about motion perception?

Corollary Discharge Model

Motion-sensitive cells signal when the visual image shifts position, and sometimes this is an accurate signal that a moving object is the stimulus. However, because the eye also can move, moving visual images are not necessarily a signal for a moving object, and the absence of a moving visual image is not necessarily a signal that no movement is occurring.

The corollary discharge model was proposed to explain how both eye movements and image movement are used together to determine whether motion is perceived. Basically, this model suggests that motion is perceived only if a comparator receives a signal from either the system carrying image movement information or the system carrying information about eye movements, but not if both systems are active.

In this exercise you will explore the corollary discharge model. By clicking on a description of a situation, the active components of the system will be highlighted and the perceptual effect will be indicated. As you test each situation, try to predict whether one (which one?) or both systems will send input to the comparator, and what the perceptual result will be.

Click SCRIPT or AUDIO for additional explanation of the corollary discharge theory.

RESULTS & DISCUSSION

1. Use the corollary discharge theory to explain the perceptual result for the first three situations.

2. Information about eye movements is sent to the brain when "stretch" receptors in the muscles are stimulated by a change in muscle tension. Why, then, is motion perceived when the eye is paralyzed, producing no movement with which to stimulate the stretch receptors, and there is no movement of the image with a stationary environment?

3. It is possible to have a stationary object, an active image movement system, and no movement of the eye muscles, and have no perception of motion? Describe a situation in which this would occur. What must be added to the corollary discharge theory to accommodate this situation?

311

Biological Motion

A few small lights placed on the joints of a person's body do not usually produce a perception of a human figure – unless the person begins to move. When movement is added, what previously was just a collection of random dots is transformed into the perception of a person. This phenomenon is called biological motion.

In this lab, you will observe biological motion. Examine the dots in their unmoving state and try to identify any form represented. Note the change in the form when motion is added. Finally, when motion ceases, pay attention to whether the lights are perceived as human figures.

RESULTS & DISCUSSION

1. Did the motionless array of dots produce any recognizable figure? Describe what you saw when motion began.

2. At the end of the segment the dots no longer moved. Did the dots still produce a perception of a person?

3. Why does motion change perception so drastically?

Motion and Introduced Occlusion

Apparent motion is not just a "bottom-up" governed phenomenon. If it were just a matter of motion sensitive cells being activated, the larger context of the display would play a very small role in the nature of the apparent motion that is perceived. That is not the case, however, as this demonstration illustrates. Here, the characteristics of the entire display play a role in the final perception. Although the objects that are presented will not change when another element is added, what you will perceive quite likely will.

Examine the two frames so that you understand the stimuli being presented. Adjust the interstimulus interval until strong apparent motion occurs. Note the type of motion you see. Next, put your finger or a piece of paper near the screen to block out a portion of the display, and note what, if any, effect this has on the motion perceived. Think about the significance of this demonstration.

RESULTS & DISCUSSION

1. Describe the apparent motion you saw with the basic stimulus arrangement. What does the second sphere do?

2. Describe the apparent motion you saw when you added your finger to the display. Explain the effect your finger had on the perception of apparent motion. Why does it make sense that this occurs?

3. Explain why this effect is very significant for models of apparent motion based on motion-sensitive cells.

Field Effects and Apparent Movement

An object added in a position that would occlude a figure's real movement causes apparent movement to be perceived, even if the figure never appears in the second, movement-inducing location. In fact, the object will be perceived to move behind the occluding stimulus, rather than simply flashing on and off.

Occlusion effects may be influenced by the characteristics of the larger field, too. How other components of the stimulus array behave impacts the perception of individual elements of the display. This exercise nicely illustrates this influence.

View each frame separately so that you understand what the two component stimuli involve. Click START to begin alternating the frames. Adjust the interstimulus interval until strong apparent movement occurs. Note how the ducks appear to move. Click INTRODUCE SIGN to add a sign to the display. Pay close attention to the duck just to the left of the sign. Notice whether it appears to move behind the sign or just flashes on and off. For another interesting effect, view the duck by the sign through a very narrow tube. The tube should be small enough that only the duck, part of the sign, and a small region above and below the "target" duck are visible. Note what you see when (1) only the "target" duck and the sign are visible; (2) when the ducks directly above and below the "target" duck are included; and (3) when the "target" duck , the sign, and only one other duck is visible.

RESULTS & DISCUSSION

1. What did you see when the sign was not included? What happened when the sign was added? Why did this occur?

2. What did you see in each of the restricted viewing conditions? Why do you think the motion was different? What do these results tell us about how apparent movement is perceived?

Context and Apparent Speed

Have you ever noticed on a rollercoaster or while driving that it seems as if you are moving faster when there are objects near by than when you are moving through a more open environment? It's true; the context in which movement occurs can significantly influence the perception of movement. The designers of thrill rides sometimes utilize this fact to maximize the experience of speed, in fact.

In this demonstration you will see a bouncing ball. Notice whether the ball's speed changes and when this change occurs. You should adjust the speed of the ball and check for variations in the effect as speed is manipulated. Think about why this effect might occur.

RESULTS & DISCUSSION

1. Describe the ball's movement and any noticeable variations in speed.

2. Did the initial speed of the ball influence whether or not variations occurred?

3. Why might context influence perceived speed? Consider the information that can signal movement.

Motion in Depth

Stereograms create a strong perception of depth by producing retinal disparity. In retinal disparity, the image of an object falls on non-corresponding points on the retina of each eye. By varying the degree and nature of the disparity, the perception of different depths may be created. Stereograms present slightly different images to each eye so that retinal disparity occurs, and thus, 3D perception.

In this exercise you will need red-green filter glasses to ensure that each eye receives only its appropriate image. With glasses on, observe the motion of the central circle, and think about how the perception relates to the stimulus.

RESULTS & DISCUSSION

1. Describe the motion you perceived.

2. How did a 2-dimensional stimulus create the perception of depth? How was disparity varied to create the motion?

Chapter 10: Perception and Action

Virtual Labs for Chapter 10:

Flow From Walking Down a Hallway
Stimuli Used in Warren Experiment

Flow From Walking Down a Hallway

Psychologists who take an ecological perspective correctly point out that the natural environment contains a rich array of cues that produce generally accurate perceptions. They also argue that the artificial environments of much research in perception strips away most of the information that is normally available to the observer, and as a result, creates an invalid view of how perception is created. Especially noteworthy, from this perspective, is the idea that perception is not limited to passive sensory reception. The observer interacts with the environment and moves through it, and this interaction provides significant information used in spatial location, object perception, and the perception of motion.

This demonstration simulates some of the information available, the optic flow, as the observer walks down a hallway. Pay special attention to the cues for motion and depth.

RESULTS & DISCUSSION

1. What kinds of information are available in the optic flow illustrated in this simulation? What does each type of information signal?

2. How are the slight changes in direction signaled? How is speed of motion signaled?

3. Would the optic flow differ when the physical environment (e.g., the walls of the hallway) moves toward the observer, compared to when the observer moves through the environment? Explain how the observer would be able to differentiate the real situation.

Stimuli Used in Warren Experiment

Research by Warren established that people can use optical flow information for perceiving their path of motion and for guiding their movement through the environment. Warren presented optic flow stimuli and had people judge the path of movement and guide their movements using this information. Warren found that people can very accurately determine the direction of the path using only optical flow information. When guiding their movements, people use not only optic flow but also other information from the environment.

In this demonstration, Warren's optic flow stimuli are presented. You will see a vertical line and random dots. For each of the three trials, try to establish the path of movement, and pay attention to the type of information that allows you to do this.

RESULTS & DISCUSSION

1. Describe the path for each of the three trials. Were the three paths equally easy to perceive?

2. What information assisted your observation? Did the information differ in the three trials?

3. What would improve your perception?

Chapter 11: Sound, The Auditory System, and Pitch Perception

Virtual Labs for Chapter 11:

Decibel Scale
Loudness Scaling
Tone Height and Tone Chroma
Frequency Response of the Ear
Harmonics of a Gong
Effect of Harmonics on Timbre
Timbre of a Piano Tone Played Backwards Masking High and Low Frequencies
Periodicity Pitch: Eliminating the Fundamental and Lower Harmonics
Periodicity Pitch: St. Martin Chimes with Harmonics Removed

Decibel Scale

The intensity of a sound stimulus is a function of its sound pressure level. To use sound pressure level in its basic form, however, is not very feasible because of the range involved. To solve this problem, a scale that is more compressed is used: the decibel (dB). The formula for dB is $dB = 20\log(p/p_0)$, where p = the sound pressure level of the stimulus, and p_0 = a standard sound pressure level. The standard sound pressure level is approximately the absolute threshold at 1000 Hz.

Because the dB scale is logarithmic, large increases in the pressure ratio result in relatively small increases in the dB SPL. For example, multiplying the pressure ratio by 10 increases dB by 20 dB. So, a change from 20 dB to 40 dB represents a change in the pressure ratio from 10 to 100, but a change from 120 dB to 140 dB occurs when the pressure ratio increases from 1 million to 10 million.

In this exercise you will hear the magnitude of change associated with increases of 10 dB SPL. For each pair of tones, the second tone will be 10 dB louder than the first. Notice whether you can hear both tones in each of the pairs and whether the increase in loudness is the same for all pairs.

RESULTS & DISCUSSION

1. Were you able to hear both tones in all five pairs of tones? Why might some people not hear all the tones?

2. The second tone in each pair was 10dB greater than the first tone. Did the change in loudness sound the same across all five pairs of tones? What does this suggest?

Loudness Scaling

Stevens' magnitude estimation procedure has commonly been used to map the relationship between physical intensity and loudness. In this procedure, observers assign a loudness rating to sounds of different physical intensities. Observers are initially presented a standard stimulus and told the rating it should be assigned, and subsequent stimuli are rated relative to that standard. By plotting the rating as a function of the physical intensity, the relationship between loudness and intensity may be identified. Once commonly cited result of such rating experiments is that an increase of 10 dB results in a perceived doubling of the intensity.

In this exercise, you will participate in a magnitude estimation procedure like that described above. Create a matrix like the one shown in the exercise. Use this matrix to record your rating for each stimulus. Six series of stimuli will be presented. The first stimulus in each series is the standard stimulus, and it should be assigned a rating of 10. Record your rating for each stimulus, scaling your rating so a stimulus that sounds twice as loud as the standard is given a rating twice as great (i.e., 20), and a loudness half that of the standard is given a rating half as great (i.e., 5). After you have completed all six series, click the NEXT arrow to see the physical intensity of the stimuli. Plot the ratings you gave as a function of the physical intensity of the stimulus.

RESULTS & DISCUSSION

1. Report your ratings for each stimulus, and plot them as a function of the physical intensity.

2. Based on the function you've plotted, does an increase in 10 dB result in a doubling of loudness? Is this true for the entire range of stimuli?

3. How consistent were your ratings? Did consistency vary across intensities, or did the inconsistent ratings occur with no predictability? What do you think accounts for any inconsistencies?

4. The stimuli in this exercise consisted of approximately "white noise," a mixture of many frequencies. Do you think your data would look different if pure tones were used? Would the frequency of the tone make a difference? Why or why not?

Tone Height and Tone Chroma

Pitch is largely determined by the dominant frequency of a tone. As frequency increases, so does pitch. Pitch does not increase in a strictly linear fashion, however. Some pitches, those separated by an octave, sound very similar. This progression has been described in terms of a spiral: increasing frequency increases the position on the vertical dimension, but the notes also circle around as they increase so that each *A,* or *B,* or *C,* etc., lies directly above the lower frequency *A, B,* or *C.*

This exercise presents stimuli that demonstrate the concept of tone height and tone chroma. Listen carefully to each series of tones, noting the differences and similarities of the stimuli in each series.

RESULTS & DISCUSSION

1. Explain what is meant by tone height. How do stimuli of differing tone height differ physically? How do they differ perceptually?

2. Explain what is meant by tone chroma. How are stimuli with the same tone chroma related? How do they differ perceptually?

3. For the accented tones in the third series, describe how they relate in terms of tone height and tone chroma. Relate this to the spiral representation of pitch described above.

Frequency Response of the Ear

The auditory receptors respond when the sound stimulus sets the cochlear fluid and membranes in motion, causing the receptors to be physically bent or shifted. Not all sound stimuli are equally effective in producing activity in the receptors, however. As a result, sensitivity varies by stimulus frequency, as the audibility curve in your text illustrates.

The audibility curve for humans is not the same for all individuals, especially when people of different ages are compared. The elderly, for example, tend to lose sensitivity to high frequencies. After being in a very noisy environment, even young people will show a temporary shift in their audibility curve. Think about how things sounded after you've left a loud rock concert or a noisy work setting.

This exercise demonstrates the variation in sensitivity across different frequencies. Before listening to the tone series, be sure to adjust the volume to a comfortable level. After adjusting the calibration tone's intensity, click on SERIES 1. Each series contains nine tones that are equal in physical intensity. Listen carefully, and record which tones in each series you can hear. Also note whether each tone in a series sounds equally loud. Repeat for SERIES 2 and 3. If you have headphones, use them.

RESULTS & DISCUSSION

1. Report the tones you could hear in each series. Compare your results for the three series and explain what you observed.

2. Did all of the tones in a series sound equally loud?

3. What does this exercise show about the relationship between physical intensity and loudness?

4. Using the information in this exercise and what you know about the audibility curve, explain why music often sounds much better when played at reasonably loud levels, rather than at low levels.

337

Harmonics of a Gong

Complex tones consist of a fundamental frequency and its harmonics. Harmonics are multiples of the fundamental frequency. So if the fundamental frequency is 500 Hz, the harmonics will be 1000 Hz, 1500 Hz, 2000 Hz, and so on. Although pure tones that consist only of a single frequency can be produced in the laboratory, most sounds in the environment are complex tones. The specific harmonics and their specific strengths produce the different sounds heard when different instruments play the same fundamental note.

In this exercise, you will hear a complex sound (a gong) presented several times. The complex sound will be preceded by a cue tone that is one of the harmonics. Listen carefully and see if you can detect the cue tone harmonic in the complex sound. Record whether or not you detect each harmonic and note when in the complex sound (e.g., beginning, middle, end) you detected the harmonic.

RESULTS & DISCUSSION

1. Which cue tones could you detect in the gong? Were some easier to hear than others? Which ones?

2. Why might some harmonics not be detected?

3. When in the complex tones did you detect each harmonic? What does this suggest?

339

Effect of Harmonics on Timbre

Although pure tones that contain only a single frequency and no harmonics can be produced by artificial means, most musical tones are composed of a fundamental frequency and its harmonics. The exact nature of the sound depends on the specific harmonics present and their relative strengths. Some instruments, like the guitar, tend to produce sounds with many harmonics of varying strengths, and others, like the flute, produce sounds with few harmonics. This variation in composition of a sound produces the auditory quality characteristic of each instrument. This characteristic is called the sound's timbre.

This lab illustrates how the number of harmonics can affect the timbre of a sound. You will hear a series of tones. The first tone will consist only of the fundamental frequency. Eight harmonics will be added to the fundamental frequency one at a time on subsequent presentations of the tone. Pay close attention to how the sound changes as the harmonics are added.

RESULTS & DISCUSSION

1. How did the sound change as harmonics were added?

2. What general conclusion might we make concerning the influence of having multiple harmonics?

3. Did pitch change as harmonics were added? Explain this.

Timbre of a Piano Tone Played Backwards

The previous lab demonstrated that the harmonic components of a tone affect timbre. The specific harmonics are not the only determinant of timbre, however. The timing of a tone's attack and decay also greatly influence timbre. Attack is the buildup of the sound at the beginning of the tone. Decay is the decrease in the sound at the end of the tone. The speed of attack and decay influences the "sound envelope," the "shape" of the sound, and apparently the nature of the sound envelope is important in timbre.

This lab demonstrates how changing the attack and decay may affect the characteristics of sounds. You will hear two versions of a composition played on the piano. In the first, the piece is played normally. Pay attention to the timbre of the piano. In the second, the notes are in the same order as the original piece, but instead of the beginning of each note coming first, the end of the sound is heard first. Again, note the timbre. Be sure you understand how the versions differ.

RESULTS & DISCUSSION

1. Compare the characteristics of each version of the music. Did timbre vary?

2. Did the pitch change when the sounds were reversed? Was the melody the same?

3. Why does the second version sound so different? (Don't just say, "The sounds are played backwards." Give specific reasons, using the characteristics of sound previously discussed.)

343

Masking High and Low Frequencies

Masking occurs when the presence of a one stimulus reduces the observer's ability to perceive or process another stimulus. Masking is not surprising if the two stimuli physically overlap, but masking also can occur when the mask and target stimulus do not overlap.

As your text points out, the results of auditory masking studies provides support for the place theory of pitch discrimination. Research shows that the effect of masking varies with the frequency of the target tone relative to the masking tone. The movement patterns for the basilar membrane are consistent with this masking effect, and thus, the masking data are interpreted as evidence for the place theory.

This exercise demonstrates the auditory masking effect found in the research described above. A 600 Hz mask is always used, but the test tone is either 200 Hz or 1000 Hz. The test tone will be presented three times during each masking tone. This will be repeated several times, with the intensity of the test tone decreased on each subsequent trial. Listen carefully and count the number of trials in which you are able to detect all three presentations of the 1000 Hz test tone. Repeat for the 200 Hz test tone. Use headphones, if possible, but be sure to adjust the volume to a comfortable level.

RESULTS & DISCUSSION

1. Report your observations for each stimulus condition. Was there any difference in the absolute threshold for the masked test tone in the two masking conditions?

2. Do you think the effect would be equally strong for any frequency of mask and target tone, as long as the tone is higher frequency than the mask? Why or why not?

3. Explain why this phenomenon, coupled with the basilar membrane data, support the place theory of pitch perception.

Periodicity Pitch: Eliminating the Fundamental and Lower Harmonics

When a key on a piano is struck, the sound produced is composed of a fundamental frequency and several harmonics. The pitch of the sound is related to the sound's fundamental frequency. As the sound's fundamental frequency increases, so does its pitch.

Although it is tempting to conclude pitch is determined by the fundamental frequency, periodicity pitch (also known as the missing fundamental effect) proves pitch perception is not quite that simple.

This exercise demonstrates the missing fundamental effect, or periodicity pitch. A series of five tones are presented. The first tone is complete. The fundamental frequency has been removed from the second tone. Each subsequent tone lacks one or more higher harmonics. Listen carefully, and note any changes in your perception of the tones. The series of tones is repeated once.

RESULTS & DISCUSSION

1. Report how each tone in the series sounded. Did the tones all sound the same? If not, how did they differ, and when did this difference first occur?

2. What does this phenomenon prove concerning how pitch is analyzed?

3. Some components of a tone may be presented to one ear, and other components presented to the other ear, and the pitch will be the same as when all components are presented to a single ear. What does this mean in terms of where pitch is analyzed?

Periodicity Pitch: St. Martin Chimes with Harmonics Removed

In the previous demonstration of periodicity pitch, the missing fundamental frequency and the lower harmonics were removed in a systematic fashion, and pitch did not change. This exercise also features periodicity pitch, but the number of missing harmonics is increased.

This exercise presents the tune played by St. Martin's chimes. Four versions are presented. In the first version all harmonics are included. For the second version the fundamental frequency (1st harmonic) has been removed. For the last two versions, additional harmonics have been removed. Listen carefully, and note any changes in the pitch or other timbre.

RESULTS & DISCUSSION

1. How did each version sound? Did pitch vary as the harmonics varied? Did other changes occur?

2. What does this demonstration suggest about pitch perception?

Chapter 12: Sound Localization and the Auditory Scene

Virtual Labs for Chapter 12:

Interaural Loudness Difference as a Cue for Sound Localization
Grouping by Similarity of Timbre: The Wessel Demonstration
Captor Tone Demonstration
Grouping by Similarity of Pitch
Grouping by Pitch and Temporal Closeness
Effect of Repetition on Grouping by Pitch
Auditory Good Continuation
Perceiving Interleaved Melodies
Layering Naturalistic Sounds
The Precedence Effect
Reverberation Time

Interaural Loudness Difference as a Cue for Sound Localization

In the visual system, images from different locations in the environment fall on different locations in the retina, and images from different depths will fall on different locations in the right and left eyes. This provides at least some direct information about the spatial location of the stimulus.

What cues are used to perceive the spatial location of an auditory stimulus? As in vision, the fact that there are two separate receptor organs in two different locations is important. The separation of the ears produces a potential cue for auditory spatial localization: interaural loudness differences. Sound intensity decreases with distance, but the separation of the ears is probably too small for simple distance to alter sound intensity significantly. However, the space between the ears is not just empty space. The ears are separated by a very solid head, and the head creates a "sound shadow" as it interrupts the sound's path and partially blocks transmission of the sound. When this occurs, the sound is lower intensity as it reaches the more distant ear. The impact of the sound shadow systematically varies with the spatial location of the sound, so interaural intensity differences may provide important information for auditory localization.

This lab illustrates the interaural loudness difference cue for spatial localization. Listen to each tone and note its perceived spatial location. If you have stereo headphones, use them.

RESULTS & DISCUSSION

1. Describe the perceived location of each tone. Relate your perception to the presentation conditions.

2. Why will intensity differences vary by location? What positions will not produce differences? Why?

3. Why can we identify the origin of sounds, even if interaural intensity differences do not occur?

Grouping by Similarity of Timbre: The Wessel Demonstration

As you have learned, one of the tasks facing the perceptual system is to organize input into objects or groups. The Gestalt psychologists proposed several basic principles that guide this process of perceptual organization. You have learned about these Gestalt principles as they apply to visual perception in a previous chapter, but they also apply to auditory perception.

In this lab, the effect of similar timbre on auditory grouping is examined. In the Wessel timbre illusion, tones are perceptually grouped based on their timbre. Read the introductory material in the exercise and make sure that you understand how the three different tone series are constructed. Listen carefully to the first series and note what you hear. Repeat for the other two series. Be sure to note what you heard and how each series differs in perceptual organization.

RESULTS & DISCUSSION

1. Describe how each tone series was constructed.

2. Describe how each tone series sounded. How did timbre influence perceptual organization?

3. What role did the speed or timing of the tones play in the perceptual effect? Why do you think it was important?

Captor Tone Demonstration

In some situations, perceptual organization of a portion of the stimuli in the stimulus array can influence the processing of other stimuli in the array. The grouped items may be considered one item to be processed, rather than as many separate entities, and this may facilitate processing of the remaining items when processing capacity is limited. Also, the grouped items, especially if they are not critical to the task at hand, may be considered almost as background, and the remaining items then become the perceptually more distinct and important "figure" to be processed. This perceptual segregation may allow more accurate or rapid processing.

In this lab, the stimulus conditions used in the experiment by Bregman and Rudnicky (see your text) will be presented. Their experiment clearly demonstrated how grouping can facilitate processing of other stimuli in the stimulus field. Your task will be to determine whether two target tones are the same as two standard tones presented previously. The target tones are presented alone, with a single distractor tone before and after, and with a series of identical distractor tones presented before and after. Note how difficult the judgment is in each of the conditions.

RESULTS & DISCUSSION

1. Report whether the target tones were the same as the standards for the different conditions. How difficult was the task in each condition?

2. Describe the perceptual effect in the third condition, and explain its influence on your ability to perform the task.

3. Do you think that the distractors in the third condition have to be a single tone repeated several times in order to produce the effect, or are there other alternatives that would be effective? Explain.

Grouping by Similarity of Pitch

We are able to organize our visual world into figure and ground with little difficulty. We use differences in location or stimulus characteristics, or motion in some cases. Perceptual organization is also a basic, necessary step in processing auditory input. Somehow, the complex sound stimulus that arrives at the ear and is transmitted to the brain must be sorted into sounds from different sources and points of origin. Although auditory localization contributes to this process, grouping may also occur when stimuli lack spatial cues. Auditory stimuli may be grouped in terms similarity, proximity, common fate, etc. – many of the same Gestalt principles applied to vision.

This lab demonstrates how the similarity of pitch may influence grouping. A series of tones of one pitch are presented, along with another series of tones that increase, and then decrease, in pitch. The tones of changing pitch begin at a lower frequency than the constant pitch tones, and eventually reach a pitch that is significantly higher than the constant pitch tones.

Note the perceptual grouping that occurs at the beginning and whether it changes as the stimulus presentation continues. Pay special attention to the pitch of the second (changing) series of tones and how it relates to any changes in grouping. Note the rhythm of the tones throughout the demonstration.

RESULTS & DISCUSSION

1. Did you hear the two streams of tones as separate groups, as one combined series, or both? What determined how the tones were grouped?

2. Did you hear the galloping effect? When did it occur? Why did it occur?

3. If you are in a room with several people speaking at the same time, when will you be able to follow the different conversations more easily?

Grouping by Pitch and Temporal Closeness

The Gestalt principles of perceptual organization provide a good starting point for predicting how a complex stimulus array will be perceived, but the final result is not always certain. When multiple principles might be applied, there may be conflict or interactions produced. One principle might dominate in one specific condition, but if stimulus conditions change, another principle might take precedence. Expectations or experience sometimes override basic Gestalt principles, also. In the auditory system, in which temporal relationships are extremely important, the timing of stimuli often will be a critical factor in the impact of other Gestalt principles.

This exercise will illustrate the importance of pitch and temporal relationships on perceptual grouping. A series of tones that vary in pitch in a systematic sequence is presented. Initially the rate of presentation is slow, but the speed increases as the series progresses. Note the perceptual grouping of the tones as a function of the rate of presentation. Consider how the different Gestalt principles interact.

RESULTS & DISCUSSION

1. Describe what you heard at the slow tempo and as tempo increased.

2. Explain this effect.

3. How do you think this effect relates to stimuli in the natural environment?

Effect of Repetition on Grouping by Pitch

The basic Gestalt principles of perceptual organization primarily involve relationships between the items in the stimulus display. We might expect that if the stimulus characteristics produce segregation of the stimuli into three groups, it might not matter if the stimulus array doubled. A reasonable prediction would be that there would then be six of the groups, with each group being the same as the original three. However, that is not necessarily what happens. Adding more stimuli to the stimulus array sometimes causes an entirely different perceptual response.

This demonstration illustrates the fact that repetition sometimes produces an entirely new perceptual organization. Sets of three tones in a high-low-high pitch pattern will be presented. Initially, two sets of the three tones will occur, but in each subsequent condition, additional sets of three tones will be added. Pay attention to how the tones are grouped and whether this changes as repetitions increase. Note when any changes in perceptual organization. After you have completed the exercise, repeat it while trying to concentrate on the tone triads to see whether attention influences perceptual organization.

RESULTS & DISCUSSION

1. Describe the perceptual organization produced in the first condition. Did the organization change as tone triplets were added? Describe the organization produced in each subsequent condition.

2. Why do you think this effect occurs?

3. Did focusing on the triplets produce an unchanging perceptual organization? If not, when did the organization change? What does this suggest?

In visual perception, small gaps in a pattern are often ignored, and the pattern is organized as if no gaps occur. For example, four lines that do not quite meet will still be perceived as a square, rather than as four separate lines. This will also occur if the four lines are broken in places by some occluding stimulus, such as another line crossing the pattern. The Gestalt principle that this illustrates is good continuation.

The principle of good continuation also occurs for auditory stimuli, as this exercise will demonstrate. You will hear stimuli that glide up and down. The glide will be interrupted by periodic gaps. The locations of the gaps are represented in the diagram in the demonstration materials. At first, the gaps will be "filled" with no sound. Next, the gaps will be filled with bursts of noise. Listen carefully and decide whether you hear the gaps or whether the glide seems unbroken. In the second stimulus sequence, a tone of one pitch will be presented, first with unfilled gaps, and then with the gaps filled with bursts of noise. Again note whether you hear the gaps.

RESULTS & DISCUSSION

1. Describe your perception of the gliding tone when the gaps were empty and when the gaps were filled with noise. Was the effect the same for the single pitch tone?

2. Explain what happened. (Don't just say the effect was produced by good continuation. Go beyond that.)

3. Describe a real-world situation in which a similar effect might occur.

Perceiving Interleaved Melodies

In an earlier lab, you observed how timing and pitch could cause different portions of a single auditory stream to be perceived as two or more separate patterns. In this exercise, the auditory stream is much more complex, but again, separation into distinct components is possible.

The "tune" in this exercise was created by alternating the notes of two familiar songs. The tune will be repeated several times. In each repetition, the two component songs will be changed so that they are less similar in overall pitch. Try to identify the component songs and note when this separation first occurred. Note when the two songs become identifiable.

RESULTS & DISCUSSION

1. When you did not know the identity of the interleaved songs? When did you begin to hear two distinct melodies? Were you able to identify both songs?

2. Was it easier to perceptually separate and recognize the two songs when you knew their identity in advance? When did two distinct melodies become apparent?

3. Could you hear both melodies at the same time, or did you need to focus on one at a time?

4. What does this demonstration tell us about auditory perceptual organization?

Layering Naturalistic Sounds

The auditory stimulus from the natural environment is often composed of many different sounds created by many different sources. This complex stimulus enters the ear as one entity, but its components are usually successfully separated and identified in an orderly fashion. Previous labs have examined some of the factors that make this possible.

In this lab you will hear several sounds from the environment, first individually, and then combined. For the combined stimuli, see if you can perceptually isolate the components. Note whether all of the sounds are equally easy to isolate.

RESULTS & DISCUSSION

1. Report your observations for the combined sounds. Which sound was most difficult to perceptually isolate and recognize?

2. Explain why this sound is harder to isolate. (Cite some of the factors previous labs have featured.)

3. This lab presented recorded sound stimuli, and thus, some of the information available to a listener in the natural environment might not be present. Give some examples of types of information that contribute to our ability to perceptually organize sounds in the natural environment.

The Precedence Effect

As you have already learned, having two receptor organs located is separate locations in space provides important cues for visual and auditory spatial localization. In another lab, the importance of interaural intensity differences as a cue for auditory localization was demonstrated. In this lab, the cue of interaural (inter-ear) time differences is explored.

Because one ear may be closer to the origin of the sound, that ear will receive the sound stimulus slightly before the other ear. The difference in timing varies predictably with the specific spatial location. As a result, interaural time differences may be utilized in auditory localization.

Listen to the series of tones and note their perceived locations. Pay attention to how the perceived location changes as the timing is varied.

RESULTS & DISCUSSION

1. Report your observations concerning each of the four timing conditions.

2. Will interaural time differences allow accurate perception of all spatial locations? Why or why not?

3. Explain why it is hard to identify the location of an ambulance or police car when you have only one car window open.

Reverberation Time

When sounds are produced in an environment with walls and other surfaces, the listener is stimulated not only by direct sound, but also by reflected sound. This indirect sound is not a copy of the original sound that arrives after some delay. The characteristics of the surfaces involved will change the physical nature of the sound. Some surfaces absorb sound, whereas others reflect it. The surface may reflect sounds at different angles relative to the listener. The distance of the surface affects the timing and intensity of indirect sounds. Some frequencies behave differently, also, so the spectral characteristics of the indirect sound may be different. It is not surprising, then, that sounds that are identical when produced do not always sound the same in different environments.

Reverberation time is a measure of indirect sound. It is the amount of time required for a sound to decrease 60dB below its original level. In this exercise, reverberation time will be varied across four presentations of a Bach fugue. Pay attention to how the sound quality changes as reverberation time increases. Note which reverberation time produces the most pleasant sound.

RESULTS & DISCUSSION

1. How did the sound quality differ in the four versions?

2. Which reverberation time produced the most attractive sound? Why?

3. Your voice sounds better when you sing in the shower than when you sing in the open room of a karaoke bar. Explain this.

Chapter 13: Speech Perception

Virtual Labs for Chapter 13:

Categorical Perception
McGurk Effect

Categorical Perception

Categorical perception occurs when stimuli are perceived in an "either-or" fashion that does not reflect the range of variation of the physical characteristics of the stimuli. There is a threshold or boundary on some physical dimension where perception changes from "A" to "B." A small change in the physical characteristics that crosses that boundary results in a major shift in perception, even though a much larger change in the physical characteristics elsewhere may not be noticeable.

One of the most famous situations in which categorical perception has been demonstrated is speech perception. Although the physical characteristics will vary gradually, some speech sounds are perceived in a categorical fashion. The categorical nature of speech perception has been used as support for certain theories of speech perception and the argument that "speech is special."

This lab demonstrates categorical perception. You will hear a series of sounds that vary gradually in some physical characteristic, but that are typically heard as one of two words. Record what you hear when each of the stimuli are presented.

RESULTS & DISCUSSION

1. Report your responses. Did your responses show the expected pattern?

2. Why is categorical perception noteworthy? What does it tell us about speech perception?

McGurk Effect

The McGurk effect occurs when the speech sounds perceived are influenced by visual information about mouth movements. When one speech sound is presented, but an observer watches the mouth movements for a different sound, the perception does not match the acoustic stimulus or the sounds that would correspond to the mouth movements. Instead, something entirely different is heard.

In this exercise you will experience the McGurk effect. Watch the video of the person's mouth as you listen to the speech sounds. Record what you hear. Next, restart the stimulus sequence, but don't look at the screen. Again, record what you hear. Finally, turn the sound off and just watch the mouth movements. Record what you think the person is saying.

RESULTS & DISCUSSION

1. Report your responses. Did you perceive the sounds the same way when you watched the mouth movements as when you simply listened? Did what you heard correspond to what the mouth movements represented?

2. What does the McGurk effect tell us about speech perception?

Chapter 14: The Cutaneous Senses

Virtual Labs for Chapter 14:

Anatomy of Skin
Gate Control System

The skin contains neurons responsible for the cutaneous senses. The receptors for touch are located at different levels of the skin, and they have different types of structures at their ends. The nature and location of the neurons are very important in determining the type of stimulus that produces the greatest response in the neuron, and also the nature of the neuron's receptive field. Understanding the nature and location of the neurons, then, is important for understanding how the cutaneous senses operate.

In this exercise you will practice identifying several structures in the cutaneous system. Drag and drop the label to the correct location. Incorrect responses won't "stick." Notice the different structures associated with the various types of receptors.

RESULTS & DISCUSSION

1. Identify and describe the five types of nerve endings shown in this exercise.

2. Why does the type of ending influence the type of stimulation to which the neuron responds?

3. If the top region of the skin is damaged and the receptors located there were destroyed, how would tactile perception change?

Gate Control System

The gate control theory of pain perception was proposed in recognition that the intensity of pain may be influenced by factors other than the intensity of the pain stimulus. Cognitive factors also play an important role, and previous theories did not adequately explain how this could occur. The gate control theory proposes that a spinal cord structure may inhibit the transmission of pain stimuli by "closing the gate." Cognitive factors exert their influence via this mechanism. The theory proposes that input from a central (brain) control system, influenced by cognitive factors, may effect this gate.

This lab is a simulation of the gate control theory of pain perception. You will see how pain stimuli, other tactile stimuli, and cognitive factors may interact to produce different levels of pain. Begin the exercise by clicking on the NOCICEPTOR (pain receptor) cell, and observe what happens at the level of the T-cell. Repeat for VIBRATE and CENTRAL CONTROL. Finally, click on MULTIPLE INPUT and activate all three of the structures, one after another, and watch what happens to the T-cell output.

RESULTS & DISCUSSION

1. Report the T-cell activity produced when there is input from one system at a time. How do you know when the "gate" is closed?

2. Report the T-cell activity produced when there is input from multiple systems. When is pain perception reduced the most?

3. Why does rubbing the skin near an injury sometimes reduce the intensity of pain? Provide information about the output of the pain system with and without the additional stimulation.

Chapter 15: The Chemical Senses

Virtual Labs for Chapter 15:

The Olfactory System
Taste System

The Olfactory System

The olfactory system provides our sense of smell. Some substances produce volatile molecules that stimulate the olfactory system. Because the chemical composition of the stimulus is critical to whether olfaction occurs, olfaction is called a chemical sense.

The receptor structures for olfaction are located in the olfactory epithelium at the top of the nasal passages. Projections of the olfactory receptor neurons extend into the mucous layer covering the olfactory epithelium. Odorant molecules make contact with the mucous layer of the olfactory epithelium, where they stimulate the olfactory receptor neurons.

Actually, there are some additional steps and structures involved in the creation of an olfactory response beyond those described above. This lab provides practice identifying the components of the olfactory system. Drag and drop the labels to their appropriate locations in the diagrams of the olfactory system. The first diagram is the most general. Click on the arrows to proceed to increasingly detailed views of the system.

RESULTS & DISCUSSION

1. How do the cilia relate to the olfactory receptor neuron? What is the olfactory receptor, and how does it differ from the olfactory receptor neuron?

2. Where does chemical stimulation produce an exchange of ions?

3. Why do you think a bad head cold affects the sense of smell? Be sure to use the olfactory structures featured in this exercise to explain.

Taste System

The taste, or gustatory, system is another chemical sense. Soluble substances stimulate the receptors in the taste system, and taste perception occurs. The chemical composition of a substance determines whether a neural response in the taste receptors will occur and what specific taste is perceived.

This lab offers a chance to practice identifying the different components of the taste system. A series of diagrams are presented, and you should drag and drop the labels to their correct locations. The diagrams become progressively detailed as you proceed through the lab. You will begin with the most general diagram of the tongue, and end up working with a detailed diagram of the taste cell.

RESULTS & DISCUSSION

1. Describe the structure of a taste bud. Where are taste buds located (be specific)?

2. Which structure contains the actual receptors for taste, and where are the receptors located in this structure? What determines whether a substance will stimulate a particular receptor?

3. Describe the sequence of events from taking a drink of orange juice to tasting that orange juice. Use the information from this exercise.

Chapter 16: Perceptual Development

No Virtual Labs for Chapter 16

Appendix A: Signal Detection: Procedure and Theory

Virtual Labs for Appendix A:

Signal Detection

Signal Detection

Traditional psychophysical methods use thresholds as measurements of sensitivity. However, these methods are always contaminated by bias. Signal detection theory recognizes that bias is inevitable, but it provides a way to separate that factor from the sensitivity measurement.

Signal detection procedures allow observers to make mistakes – two types, in fact. In the simplest form of signal detection experiment the stimulus to be detected is not presented on all trials. Observers sometimes respond that they detected the stimulus even though it was not presented (false alarm), and they sometimes respond that they did not detect a stimulus that did occur (miss). The number of false alarms depends both on the sensitivity and the response bias of the observer. Response bias establishes a response rule, or criterion, that guides responding. Sensations above the criterion produce a detection response; those below produce a no-detection response. False alarms are compared with hits (detecting a stimulus that did occur) to compute a bias-free measure of sensitivity called d' (d-prime).

This experiment uses a more complex signal detection procedure in which multiple response criteria may be defined in one set of data. You will decide whether the larger gap in a stimulus occurred on the left or right and how confident you are of your answer. Each confidence level represents a response criterion, and the hits and false alarms associated with each response criterion are used to plot an ROC curve, a measure of sensitivity. Read the information in the experiment for a more complete explanation. Also read the instructions carefully and do some practice trials. Complete all three levels of difficulty.

RESULTS & DISCUSSION

1. Report your data for each level of difficulty (provide your print-outs). Did d' differ across the three difficulty levels? Did the area under the ROC curve differ? What do these differences mean?

2. When the response criterion increased (moved from 4 to 6, for example), how did your hit and false alarm rates change? Why does this occur?

3. Assume the number of weapons discovered in airport luggage has increased 30% since the September 11 terrorist attacks. Use signal detection theory to explain the different ways these data might be interpreted.